Hashemite Kingdom of Jordan

Health Sector Study

The World Bank
Washington, D.C.

World Bank Country Studies are among the many reports originally prepared for internal use as part of the continuing analysis by the Bank of the economic and related conditions of its developing member countries and of its dialogues with the governments. Some of the reports are published in this series with the least possible delay for the use of governments and the academic, business and financial, and development communities. The typescript of this paper therefore has not been prepared in accordance with the procedures appropriate to formal printed texts, and the World Bank accepts no responsibility for errors. Some sources cited in this paper may be informal documents that are not readily available.

ISSN: 0253-2123

Library of Congress Cataloging-in-Publication Data

Hashemite Kingdom of Jordan : health sector study.
        p.   cm. — (A World Bank country study)
    This report is based on the findings of a mission which visited
Jordan in November 1995.
    Includes bibliographical references.
    ISBN 0-8213-3894-3
    1. Medical care—Jordan.   2. Medical policy—Jordan.   3. Medical
care—Jordan—Finance.   4. Health care reform—Jordan.   I. World
Bank.   II. Series.
RA395.J6H37   1997
362.1'095695—dc21   97-1137
                                                 CIP

CONTENTS

CONTENTS (CONT.)

ABSTRACT

This report presents the findings of an assessment of Jordan's health sector which was prepared jointly by the Government of Jordan and the World Bank. The study evaluates the performance of Jordan's health sector and provides recommendations for basic reforms. Health sector performance is evaluated in terms of improving the population's health status, assuring equity and access, promoting macroeconomic and microeconomic efficiency, improving the clinical effectiveness of the service delivery system, and enhancing quality and consumer satisfaction. Specific policy recommendations are developed to improve system performance along each of these dimensions and assure long-term financial sustainability of the system.

Jordan is at a cross-roads in the evolution of its health system. Passive acceptance of the status quo is likely to result in increasing costs, access gaps for vulnerable populations, wasteful excess capacity, and poor value for money in terms of health outcomes. Moreover, the rising costs of public programs driven by the epidemiological transitions, population aging, continued high rates of population growth, and clinical and economic inefficiencies in the service delivery system will hinder efforts to achieve macroeconomic stability and growth. A carefully developed and monitored reform effort could improve the health status of the population, economic efficiency, clinical effectiveness, quality, and access.

ACKNOWLEDGMENTS

This study could not have been completed without the valuable guidance provided by members of the Policy Steering Committee. The authors of the report would like to thank the members of this Committee for the information, insight, and guidance they were able, and will continue, to provide.

The composition of the *Policy Steering Committee* is as follows:

H.E. Dr. Aref Batayneh (Ministry of Health and Chair of the Committee)
Dr. Yousef Mousa Goussous (Royal Medical Services)
Dr. Nail J. Ajluni (Ministry of Health/Private Sector)
Dr. Mamoun Moh'd Amin Maabreh (Ministry of Health)
Dr. Mahmoud Abu-Khalaf (University of Jordan)
Dr. Ibrahim Hussein Al-Ali Al-Abdulla Bani Hani (Faculty of Medicine)
Mr. Zaidoun Ahmad Salim Rashdan (Ministry of Planning)
Mr. Abdul Rahman Ajlouni (Ministry of Finance)
Dr. Basem M. Dajani (Jordan Medical Association)
Mr. Issa J. Hanania (Social Security Corporation

This report is based on the findings of a mission which visited Jordan in November 1995. This report is the work of George Schieber (Mission Leader and Senior Health Financing Specialist), Gail Richardson (Health Specialist), Eduard Bos (Demographer), Mariam Claeson (Child Health Specialist), Peter Cowley (Burden of Disease Expert), Vivian Hon (Econometrician), Michael Hopkinson (Facility Rationalization Expert), Ernst Lauridsen (Pharmaceutical Specialist), James Mays (Health Financing Modeling Expert), and Robert Taylor (Management and Manpower Specialist). Jackie Perry provided editorial assistance. Fred Golladay (Principal Human Resources Economist) and Alex Preker (Senior Health Economist) were peer reviewers. This report was prepared under the overall supervision of Jacques Baudouy (Manager, MNSHD).

This study was prepared in collaboration with the Technical Working Group and PHRD Grant Administration Committee in Jordan which included: Dr. Zuheir M. Teif (Ministry of Health), Dr. Reyad Amin Al-Ali (Ministry of Health), Dr. Faris Salameh Nicola Khoury (Ministry of Health), Mr. Mazen Muatamen Khalil Imadeddin (Ministry of Health), Dr. Matasem Awamleh (Ministry of Health), Engineer Mahmoud Rawashdeh (Ministry of Planning), Dr. Musa Taha Mohammad El-Ajlouni (Royal Medical Services), Dr. Mahmoud Najeeb Nusair (Social Security Corporation), Mr. Ibrahim Alhamed Al-Duwairi (Ministry of Finance), Ms. Muna Y. M. Issa (Ministry of Health), Mr. Adel Jamil Mahmoud Al-Ali (Arab Center for Heart and Special Surgery), Dr. Hashem Y. Al-Jaddou (Jordan University of Science and Technology and Ministry of Health), Mr. Khalid Omar Al-Jadeed (Ministry of Health), Dr. Mamoun Moh'd Amin Maabreh (Ministry of Health), and Mr. Ratib Hinnawi (Ministry of Health).

CURRENCY EQUIVALENTS

Currency Unit = Jordanian Dinar (JD)
JD 1.0 = 1000 fils

JD 1.0 = US$1.41 (July 1996)
US$1.0 = JD 0.71 (July 1996)

FISCAL YEAR

January 1 - December 31

LIST OF ACRONYMS AND ABBREVIATIONS

ARI	Acute Respiratory Infections
CBR	Crude Birth Rate
CDR	Crude Death Rate
DALY	Disability Adjusted Life Year
DHS	Demographic and Health Survey
DRG	Diagnosis Related Group
EPI	Expanded Program of Immunizations
FSE	Former Socialist Economies
GDP	Gross Domestic Product
GOJ	Government of Jordan
IMR	Infant Mortality Rate
JAFPP	Jordan Association of Family Planning and Protection
JD	Jordanian Dinar
JUH	Jordan University Hospital
JUST	Jordan University of Science and Technology
MCH	Maternal and Child Health
MENA	Middle East and North Africa
MIS	Management Information System
MOH	Ministry of Health
NGO	Non-Governmental Organization
NHA	National Health Accounts
NMI	National Medical Institute
NNMR	Neonatal Mortality Rate
NPC	National Population Commission
OECD	Organization for Economic Cooperation and Development
PNMR	Post-Neonatal Mortality Rate
PPP	Purchasing Power Parity
RMS	Royal Medical Services
TFR	Total Fertility Rate
TWG	Technical Working Group
UNICEF	United Nations Children's Fund
UNRWA	United Nations Relief Works Agency
U-5MR	Under 5 Mortality Rate
US	United States
WDR	World Development Report
WHO	World Health Organization

DEFINITION OF TERMS

Contraceptive Prevalence Rate — The percentage of married women of reproductive age who are using (or whose husbands are using) any form of contraception.

Crude Birth Rate — Number of live births per year per 1,000 people.

Crude Death Rate — Number of deaths per year per 1,000 people.

Dependency Ratio — Population 14 years or under and 65 years or older as a percentage of the population aged 15 to 64 years.

Female/Male Literacy Rate — The percentage of persons aged 12 and over who can read and write.

Infant Mortality Rate — Annual deaths of infants younger than 1 year old per 1,000 live births during the same year.

Life Expectancy at Birth — The number of years a newborn child would live if subject to the age-specific mortality rates prevailing at time of birth.

Low Birth Weight — Infants whose weight at birth is less than 2,500 grams.

Maternal Mortality Rate — Number of maternal deaths per 100,000 births in a given year attributable to pregnancy, childbirth, or postpartum.

Rate of Population Growth — The rate at which a population is increasing (or decreasing) in a given year due to natural increase and net migration, expressed as a percentage of the base population.

Total Fertility Rate — The average number of children a woman will have if she experiences a given set of age-specific fertility rates throughout her lifetime. Serves as an estimate of the number of children per family.

Under-Five Mortality Rate — Annual number of deaths of children under five years of age per 1,000 live births. This figure represents the probability of dying between birth and five years of age.

EXECUTIVE SUMMARY

Background

Jordan's health sector performs well in terms of access and health outcomes, which are among the best in the region and among other middle income countries. An estimated 80 percent of Jordan's population has formal 'health insurance' coverage. Services are delivered through an extensive network of public and private facilities, and overall capacity in terms of hospital beds and physicians is high.

Jordan finances and delivers care through a complex amalgam of two major public health "insurance" programs--the Civil Insurance Program, administered by the Ministry of Health (MOH) and the Royal Medical Services (RMS), which both finance and deliver care, several other public programs including one small independent university-based public program--Jordan University Hospital (JUH), the United Nations Relief Works Agency (UNRWA), which provides services to Palestinian refugees, and a large and growing private sector. The MOH provides coverage for the poor and disabled through the Civil Insurance Program and is also the social safety net for those without coverage, since anyone can purchase services at MOH facilities at highly subsidized charges.

Need for Reform

While the system performs relatively well in terms of overall access and outcomes, it is expensive and inefficient, and there are geographic maldistributions of resources. Jordan spends an estimated 7.9 percent of its GDP ($374 in international dollars[1]) on health care, well in excess of most middle income and even some western industrialized countries. While Jordan provides coverage for its poor and disabled, an estimated 20 percent of the population lacks formal coverage, and Government subsidies for health care could be better structured to reflect ability to pay. The largely unregulated private sector accounts for over 30 percent of service delivery capacity and over half of all health spending, and its shares are growing, resulting in a two-tiered system of care. Particularly problematic is the inadequate information on private sector spending, capacity, and utilization, especially for some three thousand private physician practices. Lack of a coordinated policy apparatus and relevant data for decision-making preclude effective policy-making across Jordan's multiple public and private financing arrangements and delivery systems.

There are significant inefficiencies in the service delivery system. There is excess overall capacity as evidenced by a hospital occupancy rate of 63 percent (69 percent in the public sector and 49 percent in the private sector). Yet, there are large geographic disparities in the availability and use of services. Inappropriate hospital use results from lack of an effective

---

[1]   International dollars are Jordanian Dinars converted into U.S. dollars using a special exchange rate called a "purchasing power parity (PPP)." PPPs differ from usual exchange rates by adjusting for cross country differences in price levels.

referral system and a hospital-based orientation for treatment. The centralized allocation process for supplying and equipping facilities and paying personnel in the public sector provides few incentives for the efficient delivery of services at the individual institution level. Lack of standard treatment protocols often leads to costly inpatient treatment of conditions that could be treated on an outpatient basis and excessive use of expensive drugs. There are inefficiencies in terms of overall management, procurement, storage, distribution, pricing policies, and the rational use of pharmaceuticals, which account for over one-fourth of health spending and over two percent of GDP.

Jordan could improve the health status of its population, provide universal coverage and better access to services, improve the economic efficiency, clinical effectiveness, and quality of its delivery system, and achieve long-run financial sustainability without significant increases in expenditures. Based on estimates from a financial impact model developed for this study, Jordan could provide formal universal coverage to its uninsured population for 3-6 percent of its current expenditures. Indeed, potential savings from efficiencies in the service delivery system and pharmaceutical sector as well as additional revenue enhancements through minor changes in the financing of the MOH and RMS programs could underwrite a budget neutral major reform effort.

Undertaking reforms now would result in better value for the almost 8 percent of GDP allocated to the health sector and enable Jordan to more effectively cope with the increasing future demands that will be placed on its health sector due to population aging, the changing composition of illness toward costly chronic conditions, and the emergence of new and sophisticated medical technologies. As Jordan's population ages over the next decades, increasing financial pressure will be placed on its system. An aged person consumes 3-4 times the amount of medical care as a non-aged person. Similarly, as birth rates decline, there will be less need for maternal and child health services. To effectively deal with both the changing composition and increased demands for health services in the near future, Jordan must begin the process of transforming its current system now.

Proposed Reforms

A reform strategy for Jordan has been developed which builds upon the strengths of its present system, while addressing its weaknesses. The suggested reforms are designed to improve the performance of the financing, human and physical infrastructure bases of the public programs, while assuring effective coordination with the substantial delivery and technological capacity of the private sector. The sine qua non for an effective reform effort is the establishment of a permanent national body composed of representatives of all public programs, the private sector, and other stakeholders with a dedicated staff, policy analytic capacity, and budget with the responsibility to develop, evaluate, and implement sector wide health reform initiatives.

A proposal to establish such a body by reconstituting a modified version of Jordan's Higher Health Council has been submitted to the Government and could form the base for a coordinated major health reform effort. Once established, the Council will need to prioritize its activities among competing reform priorities. Some of the reform activities recommended below, such as developing management information systems for public facilities, have already been initiated. Others, such as medical care provider payment reforms, will need to be undertaken over a more medium term focus. Management issues including obtaining relevant data for decision-making should be given a high priority since such information is needed for effective policy-making. For example, better coordination between public and private sectors can only occur if there is more transparency, and relevant information about private sector capacity, utilization, and costs is available. Health sector reform priorities will also have to be carefully reconciled with budget priorities as the costs of different reforms will have to be weighed against their benefits in terms of improvements in health outcomes, efficiency, equity, quality, and consumer satisfaction as well as alternative non-health investments.

The principal recommended reform initiatives are:

(i) Improve management of the health sector by:

- Developing and implementing at all levels of the system management information systems and appropriate information for decision-making including national health accounts, public and private insurance coverage information, information on private sector spending, delivery capacity, and utilization, and basic epidemiological information.
- Decentralizing MOH and RMS management to the individual facility level, providing facility managers with institutional budgets, training, management information systems, as well as the responsibility and authority to effectively manage their facilities.

(ii) Obtain better value for money by:

- Developing an investment strategy based on needs and efficiency criteria as well as more effective use of combined public and private sector facilities.
- Implementing an effective referral system to assure appropriate use of services at the lowest, least costly, levels of the system.
- Developing, evaluating, and implementing new methods to pay hospitals, health centers, and physicians whereby money follows patients and medical care providers face financial incentives to use resources efficiently.
- Adopting a series of reforms in the pharmaceutical sector including generic substitution, lists of essential drugs, better forecasting of demand, and achievement of economies of scale and scope through integration of the five separate systems for procurement, storage, and distribution.

(iii) <u>Improve clinical practice, quality of care, and consumer satisfaction by:</u>

- Improving the design of facilities and the availability of appropriate staff, equipment, information systems, and supplies.
- Adopting treatment protocols for communicable and non-communicable diseases.
- Assuring more rational use of pharmaceuticals through the adoption of treatment protocols.

(iv) <u>Improve the fairness of the system and access to care by:</u>

- Providing formal coverage to the entire population.
- Spreading the financial risks associated with health services use more fairly by better basing premiums and cost-sharing on ability to pay.
- Assuring better physical access to care through coordination across programs and sector wide investment and manpower planning.

Conclusion

Jordan is at a crossroads in the evolution of its health system. Passive acceptance of the status quo is likely to result in a U.S. type system with high costs, access gaps for vulnerable populations, wasteful excess capacity, and poor value for money in terms of health outcomes. Moreover, the rising costs of public programs driven by the epidemiological transition, population aging, continued high rates of population growth, and clinical and economic inefficiencies in the service delivery system will hinder efforts to achieve macroeconomic stability and growth.

A carefully developed reform effort could improve the health status of the population, economic efficiency, clinical effectiveness, quality, and access. Savings from implementing a well designed comprehensive health reform strategy, should provide the necessary funds to provide formal universal coverage to the entire population and pay for needed health system enhancements. Moreover, such changes could help assure the long-run financial viability of the health system.

I. Introduction

Jordan is a small, lower middle-income country, with a population of 4.1 million. In 1994, its GDP was some 4.2 billion Jordanian Dinars (JD), about six billion U.S. dollars, US$1500 per capita. It has a small economy, limited natural resources, chronic water shortages, limited (5 percent) arable land, and must import virtually all energy sources. Strong Government commitments to health, education, and other social programs, have resulted in impressive social indicators. With a literacy rate of over 80 percent and a well developed human resource base, Jordan has compensated for its poor natural resource endowments by exporting its surplus labor to the oil exporting countries.[1]

The recent worldwide recession and Gulf War have adversely affected Jordan's economy, causing a major decline in income, high inflation, and an increase in unemployment and poverty. While real GDP is projected to grow at annual rates of about six percent for the next several years, in 1994 Jordan's per capita income was only about two-thirds of its 1987 level. Long-term debt in 1994 was 115 percent of GDP, a troublingly high figure. Unemployment and poverty are on the order of 15 percent.[2] As Jordan develops policies to deal with its present economic circumstances and its transition to a globally-oriented, competitive market economy, it needs to provide its citizens with an effective social safety net, which under the current economic circumstances necessitates improved efficiency and reform of existing social safety net programs including better targeting of current public subsidies.[3] This study focuses on Jordan's health sector, a sector with critical human and economic implications that currently accounts for almost 8 percent of Jordan's economy.

This joint Jordanian/World Bank Health Sector Study evaluates the performance of Jordan's health sector and provides recommendations for basic reforms. Health sector performance is evaluated in terms of improving the population's health status, assuring equity and access, promoting macroeconomic and microeconomic efficiency, improving the clinical effectiveness of the service delivery system, and enhancing quality and consumer satisfaction. Specific policy recommendations are developed to improve system performance along each of these dimensions and assure long-term financial sustainability of the system.

This study has been performed in collaboration with the Government of Jordan (GOJ). Two groups of Jordanian experts worked with a multi-disciplinary team from the Bank. A Technical Working Group (TWG) of Jordanian health experts collaborated with Bank staff to develop information, analyze policy options, and develop recommendations in the various

---

[1] For a detailed discussion of Jordan's geo-physical, political, and macroeconomic situations, see Claiming the Future: Choosing Prosperity in the Middle East and North Africa, World Bank, Washington, D.C., 1995, Peace and the Jordanian Economy, World Bank, Washington, D.C., 1994, "Country Economic Report: Consolidating Economic Adjustment and Establishing the Basis for Sustainable Growth," World Bank, Washington, D.C., August 1994, and Macroeconomy of the Middle East and North Africa: Exploiting Potential for Growth and Financial Stability, International Monetary Fund, Washington, D.C., October 1995.

[2] See World Bank, Hashemite Kingdom of Jordan: Poverty Assessment, The World Bank, Washington, D.C., 1994.

[3] See World Bank, "Jordan Country Brief," World Bank, Washington, D.C., February 1996, and "Jordan: Country Assistance Strategy," World Bank, Washington, D.C., September 8, 1995.

substantive areas. Overall policy guidance for the study was provided by a Policy Steering Committee, chaired by H.E. the Minister of Health, and composed of senior officials from the Royal Medical Services, Jordan University Hospital, the Ministries of Finance and Planning, the Social Security Corporation, and the private sector.

Jordan's health care financing and delivery system is both large and complex. In 1994, the health sector accounted for 7.9 percent of Gross Domestic Product (GDP), and health sector employment accounted for three percent of total employment. Health care is both financed and delivered through multiple public and private programs and providers with private financing accounting for over half of total health expenditures. Critical information for health policy development on mortality and morbidity, private health expenditures, and insurance coverage status was generally not available. Developing such information proved to be a major component of the study. Policy recommendations for reform of public health programs were developed on the basis of burden of illness/cost-effectiveness analyses, while options for universal health insurance coverage were developed on the basis of an economic impact model.

This report is divided into ten sections. Sections II-IV provide a detailed description and analysis of the strengths and weaknesses of the current health system. In particular, Section II analyzes Jordan's underlying demographic and epidemiological patterns. Section III describes the Jordanian health care financing and delivery system. In Section IV, the system's strengths, weakness, and need for reform are assessed.

Sections V-X provide the conceptual and empirical policy basis for health care reforms. In Section V, options for universal health insurance coverage are analyzed and cost impacts are estimated using a health sector financial impact model. In Section VI, policies to improve efficiency through medical care provider payment reforms are discussed. Section VII analyzes reforms to restructure and improve management of the delivery system, including both facilities and manpower. Section VIII provides recommendations for reform of basic health programs and clinical practice. Section IX discusses reforms of the pharmaceutical sector. Section X provides an overview of a potential reform agenda and possible next steps.

II. *Demographic and Epidemiological Situation*

Jordan's population composition and growth along with its basic epidemiological underpinnings have important implications for its present and future economic prosperity, health status of the population, and the demand/need for health and other social safety net services. Jordan's current population and epidemiological profiles are a result of both the demographic and epidemiological transitions that characterize most middle-income countries. Drastic declines in death rates and continued high birth rates along with the shifting composition of illness away from infectious diseases to non-communicable diseases shape Jordan's population and epidemiological circumstances. Table 1 contains the basic population and epidemiological indicators for Jordan and other relevant comparator countries.

						Life Expectancy		Pop. Growth
	IMR	U-5MR	TFR[4/]	CBR	CDR	Male	Female	Rate
Countries	(per 1000 live births)		(per woman)	(per 1000 pop.)		(Years)		(%)
Jordan[2/]	**34**	**39**	**4.6**	**39**	**5**	**67**	**69**	**3.6**
US	9	9	2.0	17	9	72	79	1.0
OECD	9	9	1.9	14	9	73	79	0.7
Lower-Middle[3/]	40	63	3.0	23	9	64	70	1.6
MENA[3/]	52	70	4.7	33	7	65	67	2.7
Egypt	64	86	3.8	29	8	63	65	1.8
Iran	35	54	4.9	35	7	67	68	2.6
Iraq	56	71	5.6	38	7	65	68	2.5
Kuwait	17	21	3.1	24	2	73	77	4.4
Lebanon	33	40	3.0	26	7	67	71	2.8
Morocco	66	84	3.6	28	8	62	66	2.0
Oman	29	38	7.1	43	5	68	72	4.5
Saudi Arabia	28	38	6.3	35	5	69	72	3.4
Syria	38	46	5.8	41	6	66	70	3.3
Tunisia	42	52	3.1	25	6	67	69	1.8
Turkey	53	N.A.	2.7	23	7	64	68	1.9
Yemen	117	137	7.5	49	15	50	51	3.3
UAE	18	21	4.2	23	3	73	76	2.6

Table 1: Demographic and Epidemiological Profiles for Selected Countries (1993[1/])

Notes: "N.A." = not available
1/ Or most recent year available.
2/ Data for Jordan are for 1994.
3/ Weighted average for the group, World Development Report 1995.
4/ For women 15-49, except in OECD and USA for women 15-44, Turkey from Demographic Health Survey (1993).
Source: World Bank Economic and Social Database; OECD Eco Sante Database; various Demographic and Health Surveys.

Demographic Trends

Jordan's (mid-year) 1994 population was 4.1 million. Infant and child mortality indicators are generally favorable compared with other countries in the region and with other countries at similar levels of income, although they are still high by Organization for Economic Cooperation and Development (OECD) standards. These impressive indicators are, as explained below, due in large measure to the high education level[4] and improvements in the nutritional status of the population. Despite declines in fertility in recent years (from 7-8 children per woman in the 1970s), Jordan's total fertility rate (TFR) of 4.6 children per woman is still quite

---

[4]   Participation in education and literacy rates in Jordan are among the highest in middle income countries. Equality of opportunity for girls is well established at all stages, including higher education. In 1991-92, about 50 percent of basic and secondary students were females.

high, well above the rates in neighboring Egypt, 3.8, and Turkey, 2.7, and far in excess of the 1.9 rate for the western industrialized OECD countries.

As a consequence of high fertility and moderately low mortality, the age structure shows a young population (over 40 percent is age 15 or younger), with a low crude death rate of 5 deaths per 1,000 population and a high crude birth rate of 39 births per 1,000 population (Table 1), producing a rate of natural increase of about 3.4 percent per year. With a net migration rate of 0.2 percent, overall population growth is about 3.6 percent per year, a rate well in excess of the industrialized countries and many other countries in the region and other countries with comparable income levels. Based on current demographic trends, Jordan's population is projected to increase from its current 4.1 million base to 7 million by the year 2015.[5]

Jordan's current high rate of population growth and young population have important implications for future developments. Population "momentum" as a result of increasing numbers of women entering the peak child bearing ages means that population growth will continue for decades to come, even if fertility continues to decline from its current high level. High population growth will increase the demand for public funding for education, health, and other social programs. As the large cohorts born in this decade become of working age, the overall dependency ratio will decline from its current 83 percent level to about 60 percent in 2015. As this happens, however, the number of old-age dependents will be growing, increasing the demand for all social programs, especially health care, while the lower number of newborns will be diminishing the demand for maternal and child health services. The percentage of the population age 65 and over is projected to increase from 2.7 percent in 1994 to 3.9 percent in 2015, while the population below age 15 is projected to decline from 42.4 percent to 33.6 percent.

A national population strategy was approved by Parliament in March 1996 which addresses Jordan's high rate of population growth, unmet need for family planning services, and relatively low contraceptive prevalence rate [35 percent of married women were using contraceptives in 1990, although 95 percent were familiar with various methods and knew where they could be procured[6] (See Box 1)].

---

[5] See E. Bos, "Demographic Trends in Jordan," Report from the November 1995 Mission to Jordan, World Bank, Washington, D.C., 1995.

[6] See "Jordan - Demographic and Health Survey," Ministry of Health, 1990.

Box 1. POPULATION AND FAMILY PLANNING

<u>Policy Development</u>. The principal policy board for guiding family planning program development is the National Population Commission (NPC), commissioned in 1973, yet not really activated until 1988 when the King first referred to the need for the provision of family planning services. The NPC, chaired by the Minister of Labor, includes senior representatives from the relevant ministries (ministries of Health, Islamic Affairs, etc.), the academic community, the private sector, and select non-governmental organizations (NGOs). A primary achievement of the NPC has been the preparation of a National Population Strategy for Jordan, approved by Parliament in March 1996. The new strategy has among its objectives to lower maternal deaths and infant mortality, reduce fertility, and increase the use of contraceptive methods.

<u>Provision of Family Planning Services</u>. Most family planning services are provided by NGOs (in particular the Jordanian Association for Family Planning and Protection (JAFPP), an affiliate of the International Planned Parenthood Federation), and the private sector. The contraceptive prevalence rate in 1990 was about 35 percent among currently married women (about a 30 percent increase since 1983 when the contraceptive prevalence rate was 26 percent), of which over 75 percent are using a modern method (in particular, the IUD, the pill, and female sterilization). The unmet need of family planning is estimated at 8 percent of married women wanting to delay the next birth and 15 percent wanting to prevent further childbearing.

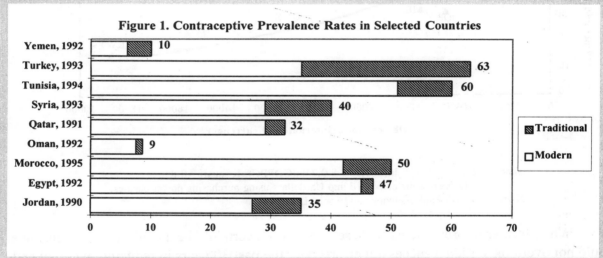

Figure 1. Contraceptive Prevalence Rates in Selected Countries

Sources: "Morocco - Demographic and Health Survey," Ministry of Health, 1995; "DHS Newsletter," Vol. 7, No. 2, Macro International Inc., 1995; "Qatar - Child Health Survey," Ministry of Health, 1991; and "Oman - Child Health Survey," Ministry of Health, 1992.

Epidemiological Profile

Providing a complete picture of Jordan's basic epidemiological profile is problematic since some 50 percent of deaths are not registered and there are few reliable indicators of morbidity.[7] However, given the major efforts to reduce maternal and child deaths as well as the

---

[7]   See P. Cowley and M. Claeson, "Public Health Interventions and Cost Effectiveness," Report from the November 1995 Mission to Jordan, World Bank, Washington, D.C., 1996.

availability and use of appropriate measurement instruments, these measures are more reliable than deaths from chronic conditions, where there has been far less policy focus.

Maternal and Child Deaths

The infant mortality rate (IMR) stands at about 34 deaths per 1,000 live births. As shown in Figure 2, Jordan's IMR is well below the level that would be predicted, based on the average relationship between per capita GDP and infant mortality found for other countries in the region. The under 5 mortality rate of 39 deaths per 1,000 live births and the maternal mortality rate of 45 deaths per 100,000 live births also compare favorably with other countries in the region.[8]

Figure 2. Jordan Compares Favorably in Infant Mortality

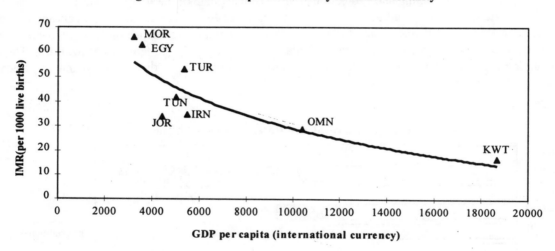

Notes: IMR predicted: $\ln(IMR) = 9.8 - 0.7*\ln(GDPPC)$, R square = 0.83.
           GDP per capita converted into US dollars using purchasing power parities.
Source: World Bank Economic and Social Data Base.

While further improvements in these rates should certainly be a major policy focus, one should not overlook Jordan's successful efforts over the past 30 years in reducing maternal and child mortality (Figure 3). The IMR has fallen from 135 in 1960 to 34 deaths per 1,000 live births in 1994. The under 5 mortality rate has also decreased significantly to 39 from 195 deaths per 1,000 live births in 1960, mainly due to declines in the child (1-4 years) mortality rate, which has decreased from 60 in 1960 to 5 deaths per 1,000 children age 1-4 years.

---

[8]   See World Bank, <u>Social Indicators of Development 1995</u>, World Bank, Washington, D.C., 1995.

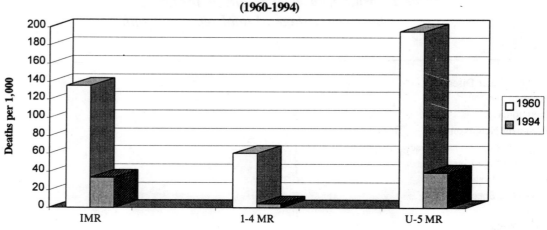

Figure 3. Improvements in Infant and Childhood Mortality (1960-1994)

Source: E. Bos, "Demographic Trends in Jordan," Report from the November 1995 Mission
to Jordan, World Bank, Washington, D.C., 1995.

These declines have occurred as a result of focused Government maternal and child health activities, and improvements in education, birth spacing, sanitation and access to clean water. Important factors for the drop in the mortality rate in ages 1-4 are increased vaccination coverage rates (fully immunized child coverage rates have doubled since 1980 from approximately 40 percent), the increased use of oral rehydration therapy, and overall better status of childhood nutrition.

Maternal deaths have also decreased, from 80 in 1979 to 45 deaths per 100,000 live births in 1993. During the same time period use of antenatal care has expanded, and about 90 percent of all births are attended by trained health personnel. Although progress has been made against maternal and infant mortality rates at the national level, there are three to one variations in these rates among governorates.[9]

Principal Causes of Death

Table 2 contains the percent distribution of the main causes of death, based on the 50 percent of deaths in Jordan that are reported.[10] As can be seen in Table 2, the leading cause of reported death in Jordan for males (44.2 percent of all reported male deaths) and females (34.5 percent of all reported deaths) are diseases of the cardiovascular system. Other important causes include accidents (particularly for males) and pneumonia. It is apparent that non-communicable diseases have become an important cause of registered deaths.

---

[9] Ministry of Health, <u>Jordan Population and Family Health Survey, 1990</u>, Ministry of Health, Amman, Jordan, August 1992, p.79.

[10] Age-specific breakdowns of the deaths were not available. There are also limitations to using these data for health policy planning; in particular, deaths in rural areas are probably under-registered at a greater frequency than in urban areas. This suggests that early childhood and perinatal deaths are under-registered at a greater frequency due to their greater prevalence in rural areas.

Table 2: Main Causes of Death in Jordan (1991) (as a percentage of total reported deaths)		
Cause of Death	Male	Female
Cardiovascular Disease	44.2%	34.5%
Accidents	15.4%	6.7%
Pneumonia	5.0%	4.0%
Malignant Neoplasm	2.2%	3.1%
Diseases of the Urinary Tract	1.9%	3.3%
Diseases of the Liver	1.2%	1.4%
Infectious Disease	0.3%	0.3%
Other (Not Specified)	29.8%	46.7%
Total	100%	100%
Total Number of Cases	6,758	4,510

Source: "Health Financing Study"; Center for Consultation, Technical Services, and Studies, University of Jordan; March 1995.

Morbidity

There are no reliable indicators of morbidity patterns in Jordan. However, utilization indicators show that the major reasons for seeking care are diseases of the respiratory system, accounting for 36 percent of all registered visits in Jordan from 1991-1994. Infectious and parasitic diseases account for 12 percent of visits, while diseases of the digestive system account for 10 percent. Other data sources indicate that musculo-skeletal (mainly arthritis) and endocrine disease cases (mainly diabetes type II) have become increasingly frequent in those age 45 and above.

Burden of Disease

One frequently used measure of the burden of disease is the disability adjusted life year (DALY) concept: a composite indicator measuring both death and disability.[11] As shown in Table 3, the greatest loss of DALYs in Jordan are a mixture of adult and very early childhood diseases.[12] The greatest single loss of DALYs in Jordan is ischemic heart disease (25.0 percent of DALYs lost), while cerebrovascular disease is second (16.8 percent of DALYs lost). Closely

---

[11] The DALY is an indicator of the time lived with the disability and the time lost due to premature mortality. Years lost from premature mortality are estimated with respect to a standard expectation of life at each age. Years lived with a disability are translated into an equivalent time loss through multiplication by a set of weights that reflect reduction in functional capacity. As such, the DALY represents an attempt to combine in a single indicator the impact of disease on mortality (through a calculation of the duration of life lost due to death) and morbidity (through an assessment of the length of time lived with a disability). See World Bank, World Development Report: Investing in Health, World Bank, Washington, D.C., 1993 and N. Homedes, "The Disability Adjusted Life Year (DALY) - Definition, Measurement and Potential Use"; Human Capital Development Working Paper No. 68; World Bank, July 1996.

[12] See Cowley and Claeson, op.cit. The total number of DALYs lost shown in Table 3 only reflects DALYs lost from a representative sample of the top causes of DALY loss and is not therefore complete. Particular omissions are neuro-psychiatric disorders and congenital abnormalities for which there are no available data. Congenital malformations are suspected to be particularly important due to the high levels of consanguineous unions.

following ischemic heart and cerebrovascular disease in relative number of DALYs lost is perinatal death and disability (12.7 percent), acute respiratory infections in children under 5 (10.8 percent), diarrhea in children under 5 (10.5 percent), and motor vehicle accidents (9.6 percent).[13] The results of the burden of disease analysis can be summarized as follows:

- The nature of acute respiratory infections in under 5 year olds and perinatal disease at the levels shown in Jordan necessitate a coordinated curative and preventive strategy for early childhood and maternal diseases, emphasizing outpatient treatment and timely referral for effective hospital-based care when needed.

- Progress has been made in reducing the reported mortality rates and DALYs lost from vaccine preventable disease, tuberculosis, and diarrhea. Nevertheless, these infectious diseases might re-emerge with their concomitant DALY loss, if efforts are not sustained in preventing and treating them.

- Non-communicable diseases and illness are becoming increasingly prevalent in Jordan. Efforts to address these non-communicable diseases in a cost-effective manner become exceedingly important as treatment costs for these diseases are likely responsible for a large and growing percentage of health care costs.

- Jordan is in the midst of the epidemiological transition with acute respiratory infections and perinatal diseases still causing a large loss of productive life.

- Jordan, like other middle income countries, may be entering into a newly documented phase of the epidemiological transition known as the "protracted polarized model," which is characterized by rapid declines in mortality, continuing high incidence of infectious diseases (despite significant reductions in their mortality rates) coupled with an increase of non-communicable diseases, unequal distributions of wealth and incomplete coverage resulting in widening gaps in health status among income groups and geographic areas (i.e., "epidemiologic polarization"), and possible re-emergence of previously eradicated epidemic diseases.[14]

---

[13] For the perinatal mortality rate only neonatal deaths were considered; stillbirths were not.

[14] See J.L. Bobadilla et al., "The Epidemiologic Transition and Health Priorities," in D. Jamison et al. (eds) Disease Control Priorities in Developing Countries, Oxford University Press, New York, 1993.

Table 3: Burden of Disease

Disease	Age Group	DALY Lost	Percent of Total
Ischemic Heart Disease	All	67,597	25.0%
Cerebrovascular Disease	All	45,381	16.8%
Perinatal	Under 1 month	34,250	12.7%
Acute Respiratory Infection	Under 5	29,280	10.8%
Diarrhea	Under 5	28,440	10.5%
Motor Vehicle Accidents	All	25,895	9.6%
COPD	All	12,165	4.5%
Maternal	Childbearing Age	8,943	3.3%
Tuberculosis	All	8,636	3.2%
Diabetes	All	2,686	1.0%
Colon Cancer	All	2,318	0.9%
Breast Cancer	Women	1,867	0.7%
Lung Cancer	All	1,584	0.6%
Cervical Cancer	Women	844	0.3%
Total		269,887	100%

Source: P. Cowley and M. Claeson, "Public Health Interventions and Cost Effectiveness," Report from the November 1995 Mission to Jordan, World Bank, Washington, D.C., 1996.

These demographic factors and their concomitant epidemiological effects have important ramifications for the design, costs and reform of the health system. Moreover, as incomes improve and urbanization increases, there is a danger of an urban health policy focus under which pre-transitional diseases that are largely rural in nature are neglected. Moreover road accidents, work-related injuries, and environmental related illnesses are likely to increase. These transition elements have important impacts on both the demand and need for services, and have important implications for government health activities as well as the financing and delivery of personal health services.

III. Health Care Financing and Delivery System

Jordan's health system is a complex amalgam of two major public programs, the Ministry of Health (MOH) and Royal Medical Services (RMS), which both finance and deliver care, some smaller public programs including several university-based programs (i.e., Jordan University (JU) and Jordan University of Science and Technology (JUST)), a large private sector in terms of both the financing and delivery of care, and several NGOs, the largest of which is the United Nations Relief Works Agency (UNRWA) which provides care to Palestinian refugees. The MOH is responsible for the separate Civil Insurance Program for civil servants as well as the usual public health activities and health system regulatory functions. The 'system' is really not a single unified system, but rather separate multiple public and private programs which both finance and deliver care. First, the overall system is described in terms of health expenditures and health sector resource inputs and their use. Second, the health sector is described in detail in terms of overall eligibility, benefits covered, financing, reimbursement of medical care providers, and the delivery system. Third, the major individual public and private programs are described.

Overview of Health Expenditures and System Resources

To fully analyze the system, in addition to qualitative information on each of the programs, quantitative information on coverage status and expenditures is needed. Unfortunately, obtaining reliable information on expenditures and insurance coverage status of the population for these programs is problematic. Jordan does not have National Health Accounts (NHA) which provide information on health expenditures by the sources of payment and type of service. Little information exists on the private sector regarding expenditures, private coverage through insurers and firms, and utilization of services by insurance status of the population. There are no official statistics on the uninsured. Furthermore, some of the public programs do not have information on the total numbers of people (including dependents) who are eligible for coverage, and the numbers of individuals with multiple coverages.

A great deal of effort has been put into developing a consistent time series data set on total, public and private health expenditures and developing a 1994 estimate of the insurance coverage status of the population. The data developed frequently depend on the assumptions made regarding demographic factors and utilization. The detailed methodology and assumptions used to develop a consistent NHA for Jordan as well as the coverage information are contained in Annex 1.

Tables 4-6 provide information on health expenditures. Table 4 provides information on health expenditures for Jordan for 1989-94 for total health expenditures as well as for each public and private program.[15] Table 5 displays the performance of Jordan's health sector over this period in terms of: total health expenditures, nominal and real per capita health spending, per capita health spending in exchange rate-based and international dollars, the health to GDP ratio, and the public share of total health spending and the overall Government budget. In Table 6 Jordan's 1994 expenditure levels are compared to those in neighboring countries and the OECD.

---

[15] Conceptually, the "other public" category includes expenditures by JUH, JUST, and other university-based health programs as well as expenditures for all non-governmental organizations (NGOs). However, except for UNRWA, data for these other NGOs were not readily available. Therefore, the "other public" category may be slightly understated.

Table 4: Health Expenditures by Source of Payment (1989-1994)
(JD Millions)

	1989	1990	1991	1992	1993	1994
Ministry of Health			59	62	84	93
Royal Medical Services			29	28	33	37
Other Public			15	19	21	25
Total Public	92	95	103	109	138	155
Private	94	90	123	138	156	177
Total	*186*	*185*	*226*	*247*	*294*	*332*

Note: Source of program breaks were not available for 1989-90 due to the formulation of the National Medical Institute (NMI), under which all public hospital spending was consolidated in one budget.

Source: J. Mays and V. Hon, "Health Financing Model for Jordan," Report from the November 1995 Mission to Jordan, World Bank, Washington, D.C., 1996.

Table 5: Economic Performance Indicators (1989-1994)

	1989	1990	1991	1992	1993	1994	Total Growth Rate (89-94)
Total Health Expenditures (million JD)	186	185	226	247	294	332	78%
Percent Public	49	52	46	44	47	47	
Public Expenditures on Health as a % of Government Budget				8	10	10	
Per Capita Health Expenditures (JD)	61	58	64	66	76	82	35%
Real Per Capita Health Expenditures (JD)	61	56	56	54	60	64	5%
Per Capita Health Expenditures (US$)	106	88	94	97	109	118	11%
Per Capita Health Expenditures (PPP$)	321	278	303	314	344	374	17%
GDP (million JD)	2372	2668	2855	3493	3811	4191	77%
Per Capita GDP (JD)	776	842	805	936	980	1039	34%
Real Per Capita GDP (JD)	776	756	688	758	770	786	1%
Per Capita GDP (US$)	1351	1268	1183	1376	1415	1486	10%
Per Capita GDP (PPP$)	4084	4009	3833	4457	4455	4723	16%
Health to GDP Ratio (%)	7.8	6.9	7.9	7.1	7.7	7.9	
Other related statistics							
PPP (JD/international dollars)	0.19	0.21	0.21	0.21	0.22	0.22	
Exchange Rates (JD/US$)	0.57	0.66	0.68	0.68	0.69	0.70	
Medical CPI (1989=100)	100	104	114	123	125	128	
GDP Deflator (1989=100)	100	111	117	123	127	132	

Notes: Conversions to US$ based on official exchange rates. Purchasing Power Parities (PPPs) are exchange rates used to convert JDs into U.S. dollars which take account of price differences across countries.

Source: J. Mays and V. Hon, "Health Financing Model for Jordan," Report from the November 1995 Mission to Jordan, World Bank, Washington, D.C., 1996, and Jordan Ministry of Finance.

Table 6: International Comparison of Health Expenditures					
	Jordan (1994)	Egypt (1991)	Turkey (1992)	OECD (1993)	US (1993)
Health to GDP Ratio (%)	7.9	4.7	3.8	8.1	14.1
Per Capita Expenditures on Health (US$)	118	30	105	1660	3299
Per Capita Expenditures on Health ($PPPs)	374	149	185	1500	3299
Public Share (%)	47	32	44	77	44

Notes: Conversions to US$ based on official exchange rates. Purchasing Power Parities (PPPs) are exchange rates used to convert JDs into U.S. dollars which take into account price differences across countries.

Sources: J. Mays and V. Hon, "Health Financing Model for Jordan," Report from the November 1995 Mission to Jordan, World Bank, Washington, D.C., 1996; Eco Sante Database; P. Berman et. al., "Egypt: Strategies for Health Sector Change," (draft paper), Harvard University, Boston, August 1995; "Turkey Health Financing Policy Options Study: Summary Report"; Australian Health Insurance Commission, Ankara, 1995.

Health Expenditures

Health expenditures in Jordan are high by any standard. In 1994, health expenditures in Jordan were an estimated JD 332 million, 7.9 percent of GDP, slightly above the 7.8 percent GDP share for 1989. Private spending accounted for 53 percent of total health expenditures up from a 51 percent share in 1989. Per capita spending was JD 82 in 1994, $118 in exchange rate deflated U.S. dollars, and $374 in international U.S. dollars, up from JD 61 per capita in 1989, $106 in exchange rate deflated dollars, and $321 in international dollars.[16] Since 1989, total nominal spending has increased by 78 percent, public spending by 68 percent, and private spending by 88 percent. Over this period, nominal GDP increased by 77 percent, slightly less than total health spending. Relative to nominal GDP, health spending has increased 4 percent per year more rapidly (i.e., the nominal elasticity of health spending relative to GDP is 1.04).[17] Adjusting for health care inflation, annual real per capita health spending (e.g., volume and intensity of services) is 5 percent higher than it was in 1989, indicating a small increase in the volume and intensity of services over this period.[18] On the other hand, real per capita GDP was essentially constant (i.e., one percent growth) over this period.[19] In summary, overall spending has increased in nominal terms over the past five years and has grown slightly more rapidly than GDP. Spending has also increased more rapidly than medical specific inflation. Nevertheless,

---

[16] Based on purchasing power parities estimated for Jordan on the basis of similar countries. Purchasing power parities are exchange rates which adjust for price level differences across countries.

[17] The elasticity of health spending with respect to GDP shows the relationship between percentage changes in GDP and percentage changes in health spending.

[18] On the other hand, if health expenditures are deflated by the GDP deflator instead of the medical care price index, real per capita health expenditures in 1994 are only 3 percent above the 1989 level.

[19] Real GDP actually grew by over 30 percent. However, growth in population resulting from high rates of population growth and the influx of Jordanians as a result of the Gulf War offset this growth.

Jordan's health spending, whether measured in per capita U.S. dollar terms or as a share of GDP, is high compared to countries of comparable income levels.

Table 7 contains information on the types of services purchased. In 1994, inpatient hospital care accounted for 36 percent of all health spending, ambulatory care 27 percent, pharmaceuticals 27 percent, and other health expenditures (i.e., public health) 10 percent.[20] Since 1989, the pharmaceuticals share has increased by 6 percentage points, while the inpatient and ambulatory shares each fell by three percentage points. The share of pharmaceutical spending is rather high by OECD standards (i.e., 14 percent of total health spending), but is comparable to other countries in the region (e.g., Turkey 26 percent, Egypt 30 percent).[21]

Table 7: Health Expenditures by Type of Service (1989-1994)						
	1989	1990	1991	1992	1993	1994
Total (JD Million)	186	185	226	247	294	332
Inpatient Hospital (%)	39	39	38	38	37	36
Ambulatory Care (%)	30	29	29	28	28	27
Pharmaceuticals (%)	21	22	23	24	25	27
Other (%)	10	10	10	10	10	10

Note: "Pharmaceuticals" includes the expenditures for all pharmaceutical products used in the sector, including those consumed on an inpatient and outpatient basis.

Source: J. Mays and V. Hon, "Health Financing Model for Jordan," Report from the November 1995 Mission to Jordan, World Bank, Washington, D.C., 1996.

Health System Resources

Table 8 and Annex 2 provide information on the physical configuration of the service delivery system in terms of personnel and facilities for the private sector and for the individual public programs. In terms of availability and use of services, Jordan has 1.6 inpatient beds per thousand population; 11 percent of the population is admitted annually to hospitals; hospital lengths of stay average 3.4 days; individuals use on average 0.4 inpatient days per year; and the hospital occupancy rate is 63 percent. Jordan has 1.6 physicians, 0.93 nurses, and 0.75 pharmacists per thousand population. One-third of Jordan's physicians are specialists.

---

[20] Some pharmaceuticals are taken to other countries and not consumed in Jordan. Conversely, some pharmaceutical products are brought into Jordan, having been purchased in other countries. The net effect of these transactions is not known.

[21] See Egypt Ministry of Health and Harvard Data for Decision-Making Project, "National Health Accounts in Egypt," Harvard University, Boston, 1995, and OECD Eco Sante Data Base, op. cit.

Category	MOH	RMS	JUH	UNRWA	Private	Other	Total	Rate per 1,000
Doctors	2,217	814	238	61	3,215	56	6,601	1.64
Dentists	239	150	220	15	1,174		1,798	0.45
Pharmacists	170	74	6	2	2,774		3,026	0.75
Nurses (RN)	1,342	822	281	36	1,272		3,753	0.93
Midwives	538	54	5	15	210		822	0.20
Practical Nurses	2,512	700	0	0	0		3,212	0.80
Nurse Assistants	2,044	1,656	220	122	539		4,581	1.14
Technicians	5,742	1,401	239	-	-	-	-	-

Table 8. Summary of Health Personnel (1994)

Source: Ministry of Health, Jordan

Jordan has experienced substantial increases in capacity since 1989. The number of hospital beds has increased by 18 percent with the largest increase in the private sector, 37 percent, compared to a public sector increase of 12 percent. While the bed to population ratio fell from 1.8 to 1.6 beds per 1,000 population, the number of hospital days per person per year was unchanged at 0.4, and the hospital occupancy rate fell from 64 to 63 percent. Over this period, the number of physicians increased by 18 percent, although the physician to population ratio declined from 1.8 physicians per 1,000 population in 1989 to 1.6 in 1994. As shown in Figure 4, Jordan's bed capacity is comparable with the MENA region and other lower middle-income countries, while its physician to population ratio is higher than most of these countries. Jordan has more physicians and fewer beds than Turkey. However, there is significant excess bed capacity as indicated by the low hospital occupancy rate. Moreover, the ratio of nurses to physicians is low, 0.7 nurses (RNs and midwives) per physician.

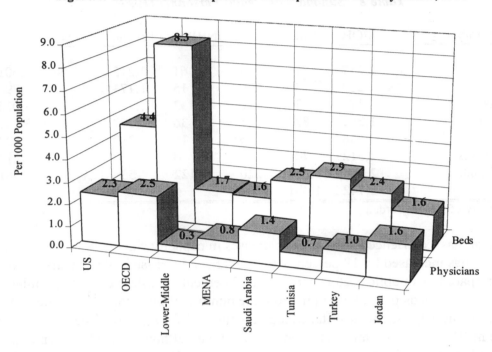

Figure 4. International Comparisons of Hospital Beds and Physicians, 1993

Note: Data are from 1993 or most recent year available.
Source: Jordan MOH, OECD and the World Bank.

Jordan's Health Sector: An Institutional Overview

Annex 3 contains a detailed description of the system and individual programs in terms of the key health sector policy parameters of eligibility, benefits, financing (i.e., revenue raising), payment of medical care providers, and the service delivery system.[22] The general observations which follow provide a summary policy overview of the characteristics of the sector.

Eligibility. Figure 5 provides a conceptual description of the eligibility status of the population, while Figure 6 provides information on coverage under each of the separate public and private programs.[23] As shown in Figure 5, the coverage situation is complicated by the fact that many individuals and their dependents are eligible for more than one program as well as the fact that many individuals with public coverage purchase private sector services through out of

---

[22]   See Center for Consultation, Technical Services, and Studies, Jordan University, "Health Financing Study," Jordan University, Amman, March 1995.

[23]   See Annex 1 for a detailed description of the derivation of the coverage shares by program.

pocket payments.[24] As shown in Figure 6, an estimated 80 percent of Jordan's population is formally covered through various public sector (68 percent) and private insurance (12 percent) programs, while 20 percent has no formal coverage. Yet, these individuals can purchase services at MOH facilities at highly subsidized prices.

Figure 5. Coverage of the Population

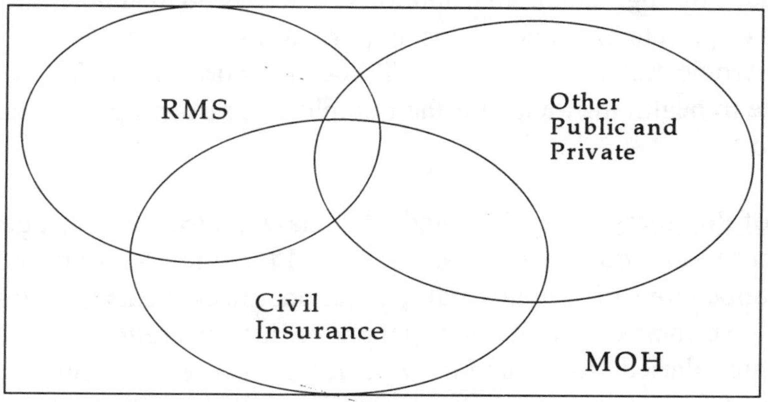

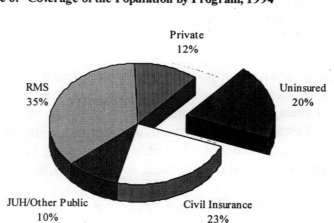

Source: World Bank and the Ministry of Health, Jordan.

Figure 6. Coverage of the Population by Program, 1994

Source: J. Mays and V. Hon, "Health Financing Model for Jordan," Report from the November 1995 Mission to Jordan, World Bank, Washington, D.C., 1996.

<u>Benefits</u>. Public programs generally cover a comprehensive array of services including pharmaceuticals with very limited patient cost-sharing. However, uninsured individuals, even those purchasing subsidized care in MOH facilities, must generally pay the full price of

---

[24] The liberal definition of dependent used by the major public programs results in many individuals being covered by more than one program.

pharmaceuticals. Private insurance benefits are more variable and the usual forms of medical underwriting (e.g., pre-existing condition exclusions) are extant.

Financing. The public programs are financed by the general budget, premium contributions, and user fees. MOH, Civil Insurance and RMS budgets are determined annually through the Government's budgeting process.[25] There are major cross-subsidies built into the budgets among public programs as well as from the General Army Budget to the RMS. UNRWA is financed through donor contributions. There is no available information on the financing sources of private insurance.[26] An important potential source of financing is through private firms via Article A.3.4 of Jordan's 1978 Social Security Law. This article provides for firms to contribute to health insurance for their employees through payroll taxes, but it has never been implemented.[27]

Payment of Providers. The MOH and RMS have centralized management systems for allocating resources to individual facilities. Individual facilities do not have budgets; rather, facilities receive allocations of supplies, equipment, pharmaceuticals, salaries, etc. from central MOH and RMS departments. Facility managers have little discretion, and health personnel in the public sector are salaried. MOH and RMS facilities also receive reimbursements based on schedules of charges from uncovered individuals. The JUH has a budget but also receives reimbursements from charges for individuals not covered through Jordan University. Private sector facilities and practitioners are reimbursed on the basis of schedules of charges. Charge schedules differ across all programs, although all must be approved by the MOH. While MOH charges are heavily subsidized, those of the other programs more closely approximate actual costs or market prices.

Delivery System. Each major program has its own delivery system, and there is little coordination among them. There is no single managerial entity responsible for the overall health system. In addition to managing the Civil Insurance System, the MOH is responsible for public health, quality, standard setting, medical education and training, etc., but beyond setting standards and approving charge schedules has little control of the private sector. Each major program has its own pharmaceutical procurement, management, and distribution system.

Major Health Care Financing and Delivery Programs

To fully understand how the 'system' works, each of the separate health financing programs is described in detail. Further discussions of these basic institutional features are

---

[25] Separate operating and capital budgets are submitted to the Ministry of Finance. Recurrent budget requests are broken down into four categories---administration, training/development, primary care, and secondary care. Each of these components is broken down in turn into three categories--salaries/allowances, operating expenses, and transfer expenditures. Capital budgets are broken down into buildings, depreciation, and equipment.

[26] See World Bank, "Report on Jordan's Insurance Sector," World Bank, Washington, D.C., April 1994.

[27] The Law created the Social Security Corporation, an independent public agency which collects payroll tax contributions from firms of 5 or more employees for retirement pensions, disability allowances, and work-related accident and injury medical expenses for their employees.

contained in the evaluation of the system's performance in Section IV as well as in the rationales for the health reforms discussed in Sections V-X below.

Ministry of Health. The largest publicly financed health insurance program in terms of expenditures is run by the Ministry of Health (MOH), which accounted for 28 percent of total health expenditures in 1994. Over 80 percent of MOH expenditures are financed through the government budget, some six percent from insurance premiums from Civil Insurance enrollees, and the remainder from user charges.[28] In addition to its general public health functions, the MOH has a dual financing function. First, it is responsible for administering the Civil Insurance Program which covers civil servants and their dependents. Individuals certified as poor, the disabled, and blood donors are also formally covered under the Civil Insurance Program, which covers a total of about 23 percent of the population.[29] Civil servants pay very low premiums (2 percent of their monthly income with a maximum contribution of JD 8 per month) and receive care in MOH primary care centers and hospitals. There is some very minor cost-sharing for pharmaceuticals and certain other services. Second, the MOH is in effect the insurer of last resort for the entire population, since any individual can come to MOH facilities and pay highly subsidized charges (15 to 20 percent of the costs) for the entire range of MOH services.[30] The MOH operates over 1,000 clinics, about 30 percent of the hospitals, 40 percent of total hospital beds, and has an occupancy rate of 67 percent. It employs one-third of all practicing physicians.

Box 2. ORGANIZATION OF THE MINISTRY OF HEALTH

Administratively, the Ministry of Health consists of a central administration located in Amman, supported by eight governorate-level offices. The governorate offices in turn are supported by district level offices at the local level. Reporting directly to the Minister of Health are the Secretary General, several advisors, and the directors of civil insurance, the information center, public relations, and office affairs. The Planning and Development Committee reports directly to the Minister as well. Reporting to the Secretary General are the Director Generals representing primary health care, curative services, general administration, Al Basheer Hospital (the largest public hospital), and the governorate health offices. The MOH employs almost 19,500 people, of which about 35 percent are in administrative positions. Policy-making, budget, and operational decisions and program management are all highly centralized.[31]

---

[28] See Jordan University "Health Financing Study," p. 15 for financing sources of MOH, RMS, and JUH. From a strict national health accounts perspective, user charges should be treated as a private expenditure purchasing a public service, not as a revenue source that finances MOH, RMS, or JUH expenditures.

[29] This figure would be higher if all poor individuals who are eligible for coverage actually enrolled and received an insurance card.

[30] This is really not very different from an insurance policy with no premium and a 15 or 20 percent cost-sharing requirement. The basic problem with this type of policy is lack of a catastrophic limit on out-of-pocket costs.

[31] Reform of MOH's organization, management, financing, and planning capacity is one of the objectives of the ongoing Health Management Project (Ln. 3574-JO). Introducing qualitative improvements in MOH's primary and hospital services and JUH's referral services is a second objective of the project.

Royal Medical Services. The second largest public program in terms of expenditures (11 percent of total expenditures in 1994), but largest in terms of individuals covered is run by the Royal Medical Services (RMS) for military personnel and their dependents. This system covers about 35 percent of the population, of whom less than 100,000 are active duty military. Some 85 percent of RMS expenditures are financed through the Government budget, 9 percent through premium payments and the remainder through user fees. Individuals pay small premiums based on rank and duty status (JD 0.75 to 1.5 per month) and receive care in RMS and MOH primary care centers and RMS hospitals. There is very minor cost-sharing for pharmaceuticals. The RMS operates 81 ambulatory care centers, 14 percent of hospitals, 24 percent of beds, and has an occupancy rate of 75 percent. It employs 12 percent of physicians.

Jordan University Hospital. In 1994, Jordan University Hospital (JUH) expenditures were on the order of 3 percent of total health spending. JUH covers its employees and dependents (less than one-half of one percent of the population), and serves as a fee for service referral center for the other public programs and private payers. The Ministries of Finance and Health and Jordan University account for about 60 percent of all financing, and user fees account for almost 40 percent. JUH accounts for 7 percent of hospital beds, has an occupancy rate of 54 percent, and employs 4 percent of physicians.[32]

United Nations Relief Works Agency. The United Nations Relief Works Agency (UNRWA) provides care to over 400,000 Palestinian refugees, many of whom are also covered through the MOH and RMS, and accounts for about 2 percent of total health spending. UNRWA runs its own system of health centers, and refers patients to MOH and private facilities for hospital care. UNRWA is financed through outside donor contributions.

Private Sector. In 1994, privately financed services accounted for an estimated 53 percent of all health spending. The private sector plays an important role in terms of both the financing and delivery of services. Many private firms provide health care coverage for their employees either through self-insuring or the purchase of private health insurance. Many individuals, including those with public coverage, purchase services privately through direct out-of-pocket payments. In terms of the service delivery system, the private sector accounts for about 55 percent of the hospitals in Jordan, 30 percent of total beds, with occupancy rates of 49 percent. In addition, the private sector employs 49 percent of all physicians, 92 percent of all pharmacists, 65 percent of all dentists, and 34 percent of all professional nurses.[33] It also contains much of the country's high tech diagnostic capacity. Thus, as in the case of financing, the private sector is a significant component of Jordan's health delivery system.

---

[32]   Other institutions, such as JUST, also provide coverage for their staff and students.

[33]   See R. Taylor, "Health Services Organization and Management," Report from the November 1995 Mission to Jordan, World Bank, Washington, D.C., 1995.

IV. Need For Reform

A rational reform strategy should build upon the strengths of the existing system, while at the same time address its weaknesses. In assessing strengths and weaknesses, one needs to determine both conceptually and, to the extent possible, empirically how well the system performs in terms of the underlying goals of improving health status, assuring equity and access, promoting the economic efficiency and clinical effectiveness of the service delivery system, and assuring quality of care and consumer satisfaction. The analysis should be dynamic, not static, focusing on impacts over the medium and long-term as well as in the short-run. Thus, both the initial impacts and the long-run sustainability of the reforms should be explicitly considered.

Defining and measuring performance in these areas is complicated. Box 3 provides an overview of the conceptual and measurement issues concerning evaluating health system performance in terms of the aforementioned goals. While the development of appropriate methodologies to measure health systems' performance is an evolving area of health policy research, such analysis should be completed even though the evaluation tools are imperfect. Analysis should be based upon the best available proxy measures and all assumptions and caveats should be clearly delineated. The bottom line in assessing performance along the dimensions described above is that one needs to rely on both quantitative and conceptual measures. Both the strengths and weaknesses of Jordan's system are evaluated along each of these dimensions.

Health Outcomes. Based on gross outcome measures such as infant mortality and life expectancy, Jordan's indicators are impressive for a lower middle-income country, both regionally and worldwide. Although there are regional disparities, maternal and child health services are generally available and used by the bulk of the population. Immunization rates are high. Nevertheless, Jordan still does not perform as well as the best middle income country performers (e.g., Chile, Costa Rica, Sri Lanka) and the industrialized countries, and as previously discussed, the high DALY losses associated with perinatal causes are indicative of problems in obstetric care and family planning. Improvements in family planning could lead to better health outcomes, particularly in terms of maternal and infant mortality.[34] Moreover, the large number of DALYs lost due to acute respiratory infections (ARI) suggests that there is room for improvement in the control of ARI. An integrated approach that would influence all major childhood diseases could result in improved health outcomes for children. The burden of disease analysis also indicates large numbers of DALYs lost due to chronic conditions including ischemic heart disease, cerebrovascular disease, chronic obstructive pulmonary disease, and diabetes, where anti-smoking, nutrition, exercise, and other preventive actions fostered through effective health promotion and consumer education programs could lead to significant improvements in the population's health.

---

[34] In addition, improvements in family planning could enhance macroeconomic efficiency. While evidence concerning population growth and macroeconomic growth is not definitive, a recent study suggests that high rates of population growth may have a negative impact on economic development. See A. Kelley and R. Schmidt, "Aggregate Population and Economic Growth Correlations: The Role of the Components of Demographic Change," Demography, November 1995.

Box 3. EVALUATING HEALTH SYSTEM PERFORMANCE

Health Status. Health status measures such as life expectancy and infant mortality are affected by social factors, not only the health system per se. Yet, these tend to be readily available measures, and comparisons among countries of similar socioeconomic circumstances as well as those that achieve the best performance are useful metrics for gauging performance in terms of health status. Burden of disease analyses, which look at potential years of life lost and disability adjusted life years, also provide measures for where to focus health programs and policies to maximize improvements in health status per dollar spent.

Equity and Access. The general principle of equity that individuals should contribute to the costs of care based on their ability to pay, but have access to services based on need is a basic normative standard used by most countries.[35] Operationalizing this concept is however another matter. Equity is generally defined in terms of the progressivity of the contributions (i.e., taxes, premiums, out-of-pocket payments) to finance health care. Access can be defined in numerous ways including financial and physical accessibility, realized access (i.e., utilization), or in terms of equality of health outcomes.[36] While some of these access indicators can be obtained from available data for the population (e.g., average number of hospital bed days, hospital admission rates, physician visits, prescriptions), generally there is little or no information about utilization by income class, since such information requires micro data and/or reliable surveys.

Economic Efficiency. Macroeconomic efficiency pertains to the total amount spent on health care and its likely implications for the general economy. Total health spending can be analyzed in a variety of ways, and can also be useful for comparisons with similar countries.[37] Microeconomic efficiency, the efficiency with which services are delivered by individual institutions to individual patients, has a number of dimensions, including the efficiency of the individual facility/service provider, efficiency of the system of all such facilities (e.g., all hospitals taken together), and the efficiency with which different services are substituted for each other (e.g., cataract surgery being performed on an outpatient as opposed to an inpatient basis). All of these types of efficiency are difficult to assess due to the problems of defining and measuring outputs, allocating costs in a multiproduct firm and measuring economies of scope.[38] One common method used to measure efficiency is to compare unit costs across facilities holding constant patient casemix. Unfortunately, many countries do not have comparative unit cost data. Moreover, even if such data were available, it would also be necessary to control for quality and consumer satisfaction.

Clinical Effectiveness. Measuring clinical effectiveness (both appropriateness and effectiveness) is difficult because of the problems in measuring health outcomes for particular interventions. Assessing medical appropriateness--whether the appropriate procedure was done for a particular patient in a given situation, and medical effectiveness--whether the procedure itself is clinically effective when provided under normal circumstances to the general population, are still evolving areas of health services research.[39]

Quality and Consumer Satisfaction. Measuring quality, whether in terms of structural standards (e.g., licensure, educational credentials), process measures, and outcomes of care is also difficult. Structural standards are the easiest to measure and outcomes are the most difficult.[40] Consumer satisfaction can be measured by surveys and the revealed preferences of consumers when they opt out of free public care and pay out of pocket for services in the private sector.

---

[35] See J. Currie, "Socio-Economic Status and Child Health: Does Public Health Insurance Narrow the Gap?" Scandinavian Journal of Economics, 97(4), 1995.

[36] See E.V. Doorslaer et al, Equity in the Finance and Delivery of Care, Oxford University Press, Oxford, 1993, and P. Musgrove, "Measurement of Equity in Health," World Health Statistics, 39(4), 1986.

[37] See G. Schieber et al., "Health System Performance in OECD Countries," Health Affairs, Summer, 1994.

[38] See J. Newhouse, "Reimbursement Under Uncertainty: What to Do if One Cannot Identify An Efficient Hospital," Report prepared for the U.S. Health Care Financing Administration, Baltimore, 1993 and S. Berki, Hospital Economics, Lexington Books, Lexington, Mass., 1972.

[39] See M. Gornick et al., "U.S. initiatives and Approaches for Outcomes and Effectiveness Research," Health Policy, 17 (1991).

[40] See Health Care Financing Review, Fall, 1994.

Equity. In assessing the "fairness" of the contribution/revenue base for financing the health system, one should consider whether individuals' contributions both through the general government revenue system and out-of-pocket are based on 'ability to pay'. The overall incidence of Jordan's general revenue structure is not progressive, since only a very limited proportion of revenues derive from progressive income taxes. In terms of individuals' contributions for services, while the Government, in effect, does potentially finance and provide subsidized care for the entire population, the structure of MOH and RMS eligibility and premiums as well as the higher payment levels required by the uninsured suggest that equity could be improved. This inequity occurs for several reasons:

- Many lower level positions in Government are not classified as civil service positions, and hence the employees are not eligible for the heavily subsidized Civil Insurance System.

- For those who are eligible for Civil Insurance and the RMS, there is a cap on premiums, so that higher income individuals pay a lower share of their income as premiums than lower paid individuals.

- The uninsured, many of whom are near poor working in non-civil service government jobs or in the private sector as self-employed individuals and/or in firms where their employers do not provide insurance, pay higher amounts of their income out-of-pocket for health care when they purchase services directly in the public and private sectors.[41]

- The fact that 68 percent of the population is covered by public programs, while 53 percent of all spending is privately financed suggests that many MOH and RMS eligibles, presumably some with lower incomes, are paying out-of-pocket for publicly covered services in the private sector.

The essence of a 'fair' system of financing is to spread the health risks of the population on the basis of ability to pay. While Jordan's MOH facilities are in effect the 'insurer of last resort,' it is clear that there is significant potential to improve the equity of the financing of health services in Jordan. Some of the options for formal universal coverage discussed below would lead to greater equity in the financing of care.

Access. As discussed above, access has many dimensions. Given that indigents are covered through the Civil Insurance Program and Jordan in effect has universal coverage due to the availability of services at highly subsidized rates in all MOH facilities, conceptually, financial access would not appear to be a major problem to obtaining needed curative care (cost-effective preventive services might be another matter).[42] In terms of physical access, Jordan has a well developed delivery system with a significant amount of capacity. Compared to other

---

[41]   Even those using subsidized MOH facilities, pay the full costs for pharmaceuticals, which account for 27 percent of health spending and are heavily subsidized for those covered by the MOH and RMS systems, as well as any high tech services not provided by the MOH.

[42]   The fact that the income eligibility level for the poor to be covered under the Civil Insurance Program is low suggests that many near-poor, who are not covered through the Civil Insurance Program, may face financial access problems even at the highly subsidized rates charged by MOH facilities.

middle income and even some industrialized countries, Jordan's health system in terms of infrastructure and physicians is well endowed. While the data on manpower and facilities indicate significant differentials among governorates, the fact that the country is relatively small geographically, means that non-emergency accessibility to facilities is generally not a problem. However, while there generally do not appear to be major financial or physical access barriers, there may be some specific groups such as the near poor and specific rural geographic areas where there are localized problems. Both universal coverage and delivery system restructuring reforms could address these problems.

Economic Efficiency. From a macroeconomic/total expenditure perspective, as a share of its GDP Jordan is spending far more on health care than other middle income countries in the region and most of the rest of the world, including many industrialized countries such as Japan (7.3 percent) and the United Kingdom (7.1 percent). Whether as a share of GDP or in per capita dollar terms, Jordan spends more than would be predicted based on the average relationships for other countries.[43] While Jordan clearly spends more than most other comparator countries, the real question is what Jordan gets for its high levels of health spending and could it get more in terms of quality (including health outcomes), access, and amenities, if the money were spent more effectively. This leads to questions about the efficiency of expenditures for public health programs and microeconomic efficiency, as well as the incentives that individual suppliers and consumers of care face. The efficiency of expenditures on health interventions is discussed below in terms of a cost-effectiveness analysis for reducing the burden of illness.

It would appear that there are inefficiencies at the microeconomic level in Jordan's health system. The totally centralized budgeting systems for running facilities, high overhead costs, the salary-based payments for physicians, lack of effective referral systems, individuals consistently by-passing lower levels of the system without penalty, little financial accountability on the part of physicians or patients for services utilized, lack of coordination among public and private delivery systems, the significant excess capacity overall but especially in the private sector (e.g., overall hospital occupancy rate of 63 percent, 69 percent in the public sector but 49 percent in the private sector), limited amounts of ambulatory surgery, little use of generic drugs, lack of treatment protocols, and future hospital bed construction plans bearing little relationship to actual needs, suggest that there are major inefficiencies in the service delivery system. Indeed, there are few, if any, incentives for efficiency on the part of any of the stakeholders.

Clinical Effectiveness. It is extremely difficult to assess how well Jordan's health care financing and delivery system performs with regard to medical appropriateness and clinical effectiveness of services rendered. The system appears to perform reasonably well in these regards, although there are no hard data, especially concerning medical appropriateness and/or case-mix adjusted mortality rates for individual hospitals and practitioners. There are impediments to clinically effective service delivery including antiquated systems for sharing patient records, lack of standard treatment protocols, small numbers and poor training of nurses,

---

[43]   See C. Murray et al, "National Health Expenditures: A Global Analysis," in C. Murray and A. Lopez (eds.), <u>Global Comparative Assessments in the Health Sector</u>, WHO, Geneva, 1994, OECD, <u>New Directions in Health Policy</u>, OECD, Paris, 1995, and World Bank <u>World Development Report: Investing in Health</u>, op.cit.

lack of involvement of hospital-based MOH physicians in both providing services and supervising physicians in primary care clinics, and high rates of inappropriate drug use.

Quality and Consumer Satisfaction. As in the case of clinical effectiveness, which is also one component of quality, there are few hard data to evaluate the quality of care and consumer satisfaction. Quality in general appears to be high and the physical condition of institutions is good. However, there are some apparent problems, especially in MOH facilities.[44] Based on structural standards, credentials and certification, there may be quality problems regarding certain physicians trained outside Jordan as well as from the small number and inadequate training of certain categories of nurses. Hospitals must be licensed, but there are no quality indicators collected that would allow comparisons of hospital outcomes or processes of care. In the MOH projects under consideration, very few appropriate standards for health facilities have been formulated. In a 1993 survey of health facilities assessing quality of care for children with diarrhea, only 11 percent of cases observed were correctly managed. Concerning consumer satisfaction, while there have not been any recent surveys of overall satisfaction with the system, a recent survey of the quality of antenatal care in MCH facilities found less than 30 percent of women satisfied with the quality of health information provided.[45] Moreover, the revealed preferences of large numbers of publicly insured individuals who chose to use the private sector for covered public services suggest a lack of consumer satisfaction with public services. Some of this may have to do with queues and/or lack of privacy in primary care clinics and some may be due to lack of confidence in some of the physicians employed by the public programs. There are no data concerning consumer satisfaction with the private sector.

Sustainability. The above strengths and weaknesses must also be considered over the medium and long-term. Will Jordan's health system be capable of adjusting to the new demands being placed by its high rate of population growth and the epidemiological transition? Can the Jordanian economy continue to support and, in the absence of efficiency gains, provide ever increasing amounts of resources for the health sector? Can cost-effective measures be taken that substantially improve health outcomes? Is the continued high rate of growth of the private sector resulting in a two-tiered system of care? In short, is the system sustainable and viable in the long-run?

Jordan is at a number of crossroads. It needs new investments, privatization, trade liberalization, and a host of other major structural changes to compete in the new global economy. This transition will place additional burdens on social safety nets due to the dislocations caused by such transitions. The health sector performs well in many regards, but is expensive and inefficient, and 20 percent of the population has no formal coverage. While health outcomes are good, they could be improved without significantly increasing expenditures. The future chronic disease burden, much of it engendered by poor individual health behaviors such as

---

[44] See M. Hopkinson, "Health Sector Study Mission: Buildings and Equipment," Report from the November 1995 Mission to Jordan, World Bank, Washington, D.C., January 1996.

[45] See R. Al-Qutob and S. Mawajdeh, "Assessment of the Quality of Prenatal Care: The Transmission of Information to Pregnant Women in Maternal and Child Health Centers in Jordan," International Quarterly of Community Health Education, Vol. 13(1), 1992.

smoking, poor eating habits, etc. is a potential time bomb of future health care costs. The rapid growth of a largely unregulated private sector and the increasingly budget constrained public sector runs the risk of turning Jordan into a U.S. like situation, whereby the poor get second class care in the public system, while the bulk of the population pays ever increasing amounts in an unregulated private sector.

The reform agenda discussed below is designed to build upon the strengths of both the public and private sectors, improve access and equity, and promote economic efficiency, clinical effectiveness, quality, consumer satisfaction, and long-run financial sustainability. Given Jordan's impressive infrastructure and capabilities, a carefully implemented reform strategy can achieve most of these goals. The five basic reform areas discussed are: universal coverage and financing, medical care provider payment, the service delivery system, health programs and clinical practice, and the pharmaceutical sector. All these areas interact, so that undertaking multiple reforms could enhance the impacts of the individual reforms (e.g., provider payment and delivery system restructuring).

V. Financing Universal Coverage

Developing, evaluating, and implementing universal coverage policies is a complex and highly political undertaking with major economic implications. For this study, a financial impact model to assess such economic inputs was developed and used to analyze two universal coverage options for Jordan in order to illustrate the types of issues and analyses that would need to be addressed should the Government decide to proceed with a major reform effort in this area. The results are dependent on the basic assumptions made concerning behavioral response and the underlying data. Given the data gaps, the results of this exercise should be regarded as illustrative. Implementation of a universal coverage program would require additional research and analysis.

Rationale for Universal Coverage

Universal coverage is a basic goal of all health systems. All OECD countries with the exceptions of the U.S., Mexico, and Turkey have achieved this goal, and universal coverage was one of the principal achievements of the health systems of the former socialist economies (FSE). As discussed above, an estimated 80 percent of Jordan's population have formal coverage through the public and private sectors. Moreover, one could argue that Jordan provides universal coverage to its entire population, since the entire population has access to MOH facilities at highly subsidized charges, making the MOH the insurer of last resort. In effect the MOH provides "an insurance policy" with no premiums and a 15 to 20 coinsurance (i.e., the percent of the actual service costs paid by the individual). The remainder of the costs are financed through the MOH Budget, and hence through the general government budget.

This arrangement, however, is not ideal for a number of reasons. First, many uninsured are near-poor, and paying out-of-pocket may impose financial hardships. Second, as a result, many individuals will purchase services only when they are quite ill, resulting in higher expenses than if the illness had been prevented or treated at an earlier stage. Moreover, individuals will likely forego cost-effective preventive services. Third, since there is no limit on out-of-pocket payments, there is no protection against catastrophic illness costs, which indeed is the basic purpose of health insurance. Fourth, as discussed above, a disproportionate share of the subsidies may be inequitably targeted to higher income groups.[46]

Given the already high subsidies to the uninsured who use MOH facilities, the low contribution levels in terms of premiums and cost-sharing of those covered under the Civil Insurance and RMS systems, the lack of an equitable relationship between these payments and ability to pay, and the current high level of health spending, Jordan could improve the equity of its financing systems and provide formal universal coverage to its entire population at little additional cost.[47] Indeed, some or all of the needed revenue increase could be obtained through relatively small changes in the Civil Insurance and RMS premium and cost-sharing structures, changes in the MOH charge schedules, and/or, as explained below, through efficiency gains in the service delivery system and pharmaceutical sector.

Modeling Alternative Approaches to Universal Coverage

To assist the GOJ in its decision-making, an economic model to assess the cost impacts of alternative universal coverage approaches was developed. Three types of costs are examined through the model: individual program costs, net government costs, and societal costs. Individual program costs are defined as the total expenditures of the individual insuring agency (new or existing). Net government costs represent the change in total government spending after the new program is implemented. Societal costs are the change in total spending for medical care, irrespective of who pays for it.

The model calculates these costs in the following manner. Baseline health expenditures are established using a NHA framework, whereby health expenditures are categorized by the source of payment (i.e., Civil Insurance, RMS, other public, private out-of-pocket, other private) and type of service (e.g., hospitals, primary care, drugs, other). Per capita expenditures for individuals covered under each of these arrangements are calculated. A universal coverage scenario is specified and individuals are "moved" into different program categories on the basis of that scenario. The 'costs' of these movements are based on three factors: induction, payment rate, and efficiency impacts. The induction impact is the change in spending caused by the change in the individual's out-of pocket expenses associated with receiving services under the new scenario. Provider payment effects are expenditure changes resulting from shifting services among providers who have different price levels (e.g., MOH hospitals to private hospitals). Efficiency impacts result from changes in efficiency of providers as a result of reforms (e.g., movements from overutilized to underutilized facilities, from inpatient to outpatient care).

---

[46]   There is a special fund for medically needy individuals allocated by the Crown Prince. However, the amounts involved are a relatively small share of overall health expenditures and their incidence by income class is unknown.

[47]   It could also improve economic efficiency especially regarding pharmaceuticals by having more effective and appropriate cost-sharing structures.

Individual insurance program, net government, and total societal costs for that scenario are then determined. The model is described in detail in Annex 1.

Universal Coverage Options

The next step in analyzing various approaches for universal coverage is the specification of relevant policy options. Given Jordan's high rate of formal coverage, the MOH already being the insurer of last resort for the population at large, Jordan's own recent internal focus on incremental reforms,[48] and the generally greater political acceptability of incremental as opposed to radical reforms, one reasonable approach for Jordan is to design the options through extensions of existing financing arrangements. This has the advantage of building upon an already strong base, while reducing the potential for major redistributions of expenditures among government program budgets, individuals' out-of-pocket costs, and private sector employers. While this is the approach followed in this study, the financial impact model could be used to analyze the effects of a far broader range of options.

Two universal coverage options are analyzed:

(i)   Allowing (or requiring) all uninsured to purchase coverage through the Civil Insurance System, and

(ii)   Implementing Section A.3.4 of the Social Security Law requiring firms with more than five employees to provide health insurance coverage for their employees. The remaining uninsured could purchase insurance through the Civil Insurance System.

Under each of these options, there are numerous policy decisions that need to be made. Some are specific to the option and others apply to both. For example, the model assumes in both cases that there is sufficient excess capacity in the system to absorb the increased demand at current average costs (i.e., the supply elasticity is infinite). Another difficult policy issue that affects both options is whether the insurance coverage decision for the uninsured is voluntary or mandatory. Making enrollment mandatory has certain advantages including assuring universal coverage and preventing selection bias (i.e., individuals enrolling only when they are ill, driving up costs to the government). It has the disadvantage of appearing coercive and further necessitates some enforcement mechanism and/or strong incentives for individuals to 'voluntarily' enroll (e.g., withholding drivers licenses, eliminating most or all of the subsidy element from MOH charge schedules). Another issue that affects both options, although more particularly the first, is the expected response from individuals who have private insurance. While it is possible that these individuals might drop such coverage to buy the less expensive public insurance, it is assumed that these individuals maintain their private coverage since it presumably provides access to higher quality services with less queuing. Nonetheless, the cost

---

[48]   See Center for Consultations, Technical Services, and Studies, <u>Application of Health Insurance Schemes for Participants in the Social Security System</u>, University of Jordan, Amman, 1994, and Jordan Ministry of Health, "Health Insurance for Jordanian Pre-School Children," unpublished memo, MOH, Amman, 1995.

impacts can be calculated under any set of assumptions, from nobody switching to the public program to everybody switching.

Universal Coverage through the Civil Insurance System

Providing universal coverage for the uninsured through the Civil Insurance System means that these individuals would change their status of paying out-of-pocket for MOH, RMS, JUH, and private services to paying insurance premiums and very minor cost-sharing under the Civil Insurance System. It is assumed for purposes of this scenario that the MOH premiums and cost-sharing are not changed.[49] It is further assumed that all the uninsured would be covered under the Civil Insurance System. Annex 1 contains a detailed explanation of the expenditure changes due to induction, payment rate, and efficiency impacts. Table 9 summarizes the changes in expenditures in terms of total expenditure changes, net government costs, and changes in out-of-pocket costs assuming the uninsured currently account for 15, 20, or 25 percent of the population.

Table 9: Cost of Providing Coverage to the Uninsured through Civil Insurance

Expenditures (JD million)	Percent Uninsured		
	15	20	25
Current Law Total	332	332	332
Total Under Option	342	345	348
Current Law For Uninsured	32	43	54
Future Law For Uninsured	42	56	70
Change in Total	10	13	16
Change in Out of Pocket	-12	-17	-21
Change in MOH	22	30	37
Change in MOH Premiums	3	4	5
Net Change in MOH	19	26	32

Source: J. Mays and V. Hon, "Health Financing Model for Jordan," Report from the November 1995 Mission to Jordan, World Bank, Washington, D.C., 1996.

As shown in Table 9, total costs attributable to the (assumed 20 percent) uninsured under the new program would be JD 56 million, an increase (societal costs) of JD 13 million from the JD 43 million current law (i.e., the current coverage situation under existing institutional and legal arrangements) level of expenditures for the uninsured. The JD 30 million increase for government program (MOH) costs would be for additional services (mostly pharmaceuticals). This outlay increase would be partially offset by JD 4 million in increased premium revenues

---

[49] The model could also estimate the impacts of such changes. In fact, given the low levels of both premiums and cost-sharing, as indicated above, the Government may want to consider some minor increases to offset the increased costs of universal coverage and/or upgrading the MOH and RMS systems.

from the newly insured population, thus increasing net government outlays (new expenditures minus new premiums) by JD 26 million. Out-of-pocket payments for the uninsured would decrease by JD 17 million. The basic point here is that providing formal universal coverage through the MOH system to the uninsured will increase total health expenditures in Jordan from JD 332 million to JD 345 million, an increase of only four percent.

Alternative baseline assumptions are possible. For example, if the uninsured were 15 instead of 20 percent of the population, total (societal) health spending would increase by only JD 10 million, and government program (MOH) expenditures would increase by JD 22 million (with a premium revenue increase of JD 3 million). On the other hand, if the uninsured were 25 percent of the population, total (societal) spending would increase by JD 16 million, and government program (MOH) spending would increase by JD 37 million (with a premium revenue increase of JD 5 million).

Universal Coverage through the Social Security Law

Estimating the impacts of assuring universal coverage through implementation of the Social Security Law and purchase of insurance through the Civil Insurance System for the residual uninsured population is more complex. Several important assumptions need to be made concerning such issues as: whether employers will be required to purchase the Civil Insurance 'package,' private insurance, or self-insure; whether coverage through Social Security will be primary when individuals are eligible for multiple programs; whether the coverage will include only workers and/or their families as well, etc. Moreover, to estimate the cost implications across Government and private sector programs, information on multiple coverages will be necessary. These issues and assumptions are discussed in detail in Annex 1.

Table 10 contains the model results for this option assuming firms are required to purchase coverage only for their currently uninsured workers and dependents. It is assumed that in 80 percent of the cases MOH Civil Insurance is purchased by firms at its full actuarial cost, while firms purchase private insurance for the remaining 20 percent.[50] All residual uninsured (i.e., those not employed in Social Security covered firms) are assumed to purchase insurance through the MOH at the subsidized Civil Insurance premium rates. The total cost of covering the (assumed 20 percent) uninsured under this approach is JD 58 million, an increase in total health expenditures (societal costs) of JD 15 million. Out-of-pocket costs for the uninsured will fall by JD 17 million, while expenditures on their behalf from other public programs (including Social Security covered firms)[51] will increase by JD 9 million. Expenditures by the MOH will increase by JD 23 million, but JD 9 million in additional premium revenues will result in a net outlay increase of only JD 14 million.

---

[50] Since firms are required by a public law to provide health insurance to their uninsured employees, expenditures on their part are considered a public expenditure (i.e., "other public" in the tables). However, when firms purchase insurance through the MOH, the ultimate source of the expenditure is the MOH, although the premiums paid by these firms will be a revenue to the MOH. Thus, when firms purchase private insurance for their employees the source of expenditure is considered "other public," but when the firm purchases MOH insurance, the source of the expenditure is MOH.

[51] Since firms are mandated by a public law to undertake this spending for health insurance, it is considered a public expenditure.

While this net increase in health expenditures, total expenditures on the uninsured, and the impacts on out-of-pocket spending for the uninsured are quite comparable to those under the previous scenario, there are different redistributions of spending across Government programs, and an increase in health spending by firms. Total health spending increases slightly more (i.e., JD 15 million versus JD 13 million) under this option than the previous one, because firms purchase some of their coverage through the more expensive private sector. The net effect (i.e., expenditure increases minus additional premium revenues) for the MOH is less under this option (e.g., JD 14 million versus JD 26 million), because it is assumed that firms will pay the MOH the full actuarial premium costs of coverage for their workers, while under the previous option it was assumed that all the uninsured would pay the subsidized Civil Insurance premium rate.[52]

Table 10: Cost of Providing Coverage to the Uninsured through Social Security and Civil Insurance

Expenditures (JD million)	Percent Uninsured		
	15	20	25
Current Law Total	332	332	332
Total Under Option	344	347	350
Current Law For Uninsured	32	43	54
Future Law For Uninsured	44	58	72
Change in Total	12	15	18
Change in Out of Pocket	-12	-17	-21
Change for Other Public	9	9	9
Change in MOH	15	23	30
Change in MOH Premiums	7	9	11
Net Change in MOH	8	14	19
Firm Contributions for Premiums	14	15	16

Source: J. Mays and V. Hon, "Health Financing Model for Jordan," Report from the November 1995 Mission to Jordan, World Bank, Washington, D.C., 1996.

Providing formal coverage to the uninsured under this option, relative to the previous option, shifts some of these costs to firms, while the MOH receives substantially more premium revenues. The necessary contributions by firms for MOH and private insurance premiums would be about JD 14-16 million, on the order of 15 percent of their gross payrolls. The effect that this will have on the financial viability of firms and the possible need for exemptions and/or subsidies for certain firms would have to be carefully studied, in particular to see if certain firms are disproportionately impacted. Employer mandates, such as this proposed option, affect both labor costs and employee compensation. In the short run, the cost of labor will be driven up, potentially affecting both employment levels and the competitiveness of Jordan's firms. Over the longer term, one must also consider that the incidence of employer mandated health

---

[52] Under the Social Security option, only the residual uninsured (i.e., those not covered through firms) pay the subsidized MOH Civil Insurance premium rate.

insurance benefits is on the workers themselves. In other words, over the long-run firms will treat their mandated health insurance contributions as compensation to labor, and future money wage increases will be offset by the costs of these health insurance benefits. The fairness of such an approach depends on the incidence of its financing basis relative to the incidence of the financing of other universal coverage strategies.

The above analysis indicates that Jordan could provide formal universal coverage to its population for a 3-6 percent increase in its current total health expenditures. Impacts on the Government's budget depend on which options are chosen and possible changes in premium and cost-sharing structures. The modest level of additional revenues needed to finance the uninsured would suggest that such a policy is feasible and could possibly be self-financed through either changes in the current financing arrangements and/or savings from system restructuring and pharmaceutical policies as discussed below. However, a GOJ decision to make policy changes in this area should be based on a detailed analysis of financial, employment, and political implications as well as implementation issues. The additional administrative costs and administrative feasibility of such options must also be explicitly considered. As the above analysis indicates, assessing the impacts of such policy changes is complex, and the analysis is only as good as the basic underlying information and assumptions.

VI. *Reform of Medical Care Provider Payment Systems*

The methods used to pay medical care providers have important consequences for access as well as the economic efficiency, clinical effectiveness, and quality of the service delivery system. The incentives faced by hospital and clinic managers, physicians, and other health personnel as a result of both the methods and levels of payment have important implications for which services are provided, the quantity of services provided, and their quality. The incentives embodied in provider payment systems must be evaluated in terms of their impacts on individual providers (e.g., hospital managers, physicians), across different provider/service types (e.g., inpatient verses outpatient care), across different programs/sectors (e.g., MOH, RMS, JUH, private sector providers), and on individual beneficiaries (e.g., extra-billing, indemnity versus direct payment of providers).

Ideally payment methods and rates should reflect the real resource costs of providing services, promote social objectives (such as encouraging immunizations), assure beneficiary access to services, encourage (or at least not discourage) quality, contribute to both micro efficiency and macro cost containment goals, and promote long-term financial sustainability of the health system. It is generally difficult to pursue all these goals simultaneously. Moreover, designing such payment systems requires underlying management information (MIS) and quality assurance systems.

Jordan's current system in terms of lack of coordination across different public and private programs, limited regulation of, and lack of information on, the private sector, rigid centralized budgeting processes in the MOH and RMS, and lack of incentives (financial and otherwise) to provide care at the lowest, least costly, levels of the system result in inefficiency within and across programs, and across provider and service types. Box 4 contains several 'lessons' from the experiences of OECD countries that are quite germane for a Jordanian reform agenda. Figure 7 displays the flows of funds to Jordan's medical care providers and illustrates the problems of assuring efficiency under the current system.

Box 4. PROVIDER PAYMENT REFORM LESSONS FROM OECD COUNTRIES

- It is easier to expand access and develop system infrastructure than to reduce capacity and control costs.
- Macro cost containment strategies have often not resulted in micro efficiency, and conversely.
- Empowering consumers and having money follow patients within the context of an overall budget appear to be the preferred strategies for controlling costs.
- Specific medical care provider payment strategies, such as certain types of managed care, Diagnostic Related Groups (DRGs), and various full and partial risk sharing approaches, if implemented properly, appear to control costs without compromising quality and access.
- When payment reforms are imposed in one part of the health sector, expenditures and access in other substitute and complementary sectors must be monitored.
- Payment mechanisms used in OECD countries require sophisticated administrative and information structures.
- Fragmented fee-for-service systems, like what exists in the U.S., without a single payer or set of rules applying to the whole system, have been the least successful in controlling costs.[53]

Figure 7. Flow of Funds in Jordan

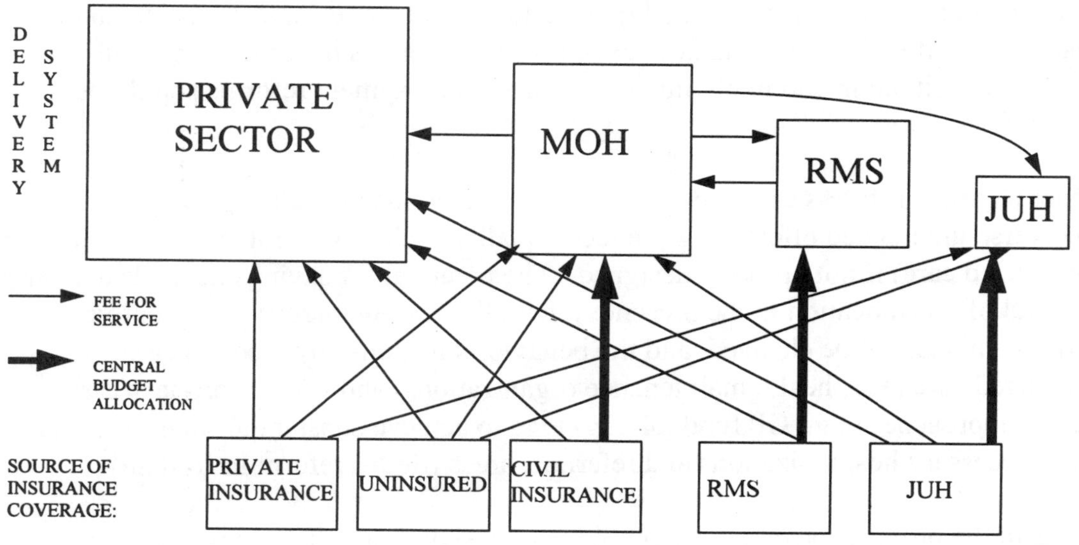

Source: The World Bank and the Ministry of Health, Jordan.

---

[53] See G. Schieber, "Preconditions for Health Reform: Experiences From the OECD Countries," Health Policy, (32), 1995; OECD, The Reform of Health Care: A Comparative Analysis of Seven OECD Countries, OECD, Paris, 1992; and OECD, The Reform of Health Care Systems: A Review of Seventeen Countries, OECD, Paris, 1994.

A medical care provider payment reform strategy for Jordan must deal with a number of issues, some relevant to the public sector and others pertinent to the entire system. These include:

- Establish budgets at the institutional level to provide individual public hospital and clinic managers with the autonomy, authority, and responsibility as well as appropriate incentives to efficiently allocate the resources at their disposal.
- Provide facility managers, physicians, and other personnel with the training and information systems needed for effective decision-making.
- Implement payment systems for hospitals, clinics, and physicians that promote efficiency, clinical effectiveness, access, and quality.
- Promote efficiency across service types by putting primary care physicians at financial risk for referral services, while assuring an effective referral network.
- Promote efficiency across all public and private sector "insurance" programs by either establishing a single set of payment rules for all programs and/or more effectively coordinating reimbursement procedures to prevent cost-shifting among programs and self-pay patients.

Rigid centrally controlled systems such as Jordan's, those in many Latin American countries, and all the FSE have not led to efficiency. Virtually all these other countries are breaking the link between financing and provision, and adopting systems in which money follows patients and providers have financial incentives to provide services efficiently. Use of primary care physicians as gatekeepers is increasingly gaining ground in many countries and is the underlying tenet in managed care. Advanced industrialized countries such as the U.K. and Sweden are following this course of action. One other related area that needs to be addressed in any provider payment reform effort is medical malpractice. While defensive medicine and cost escalating malpractice litigation do not appear to be serious problems in Jordan, a careful analysis of the current situation and likely impacts of proposed payment reforms should be included in the reform effort.

Provider payment reforms can lead to significant reductions in health spending. They can also lead to perverse unintended effects (e.g., reduced quality, lack of referrals for medically necessary specialized care) if not properly designed. The potential for savings depends to a large extent on the level of misallocation in the present system, the current underlying incentive structure, how incentives will be changed, and the behavioral response by medical care providers. Managed care (e.g., health maintenance organizations) and various primary care partial capitation approaches (e.g., GP fundholding) tend to achieve substantial savings through reductions in unnecessary hospitalizations and referrals, areas rife for reform in Jordan.[54]

Reforms in the provider payment area could lead to significant efficiency gains for Jordan, improve long-run financial viability of the system, and could also reinforce needed

---

[54] See H. Luft, "Health Maintenance Organizations: Is the United States Experience Applicable Elsewhere"? in Health: Quality and Choice, OECD, Paris, 1994, for a discussion of the applicability of the U.S. health maintenance organization concept to other countries.

changes in the service delivery system. However, provider payment systems are complex to design and implement, must be accompanied by appropriate training of facility managers, physicians, and government personnel, and must be complemented with appropriate MIS and quality assurance systems. One approach for pursuing such payment reforms could be establishing a government-wide task force including facility managers, private sector practitioners, accounting experts, economists, etc., and relevant local and foreign experts, to design appropriate payment, MIS, and quality assurance systems, piloting these systems in specific facilities and/or geographic areas, and implementing the new systems by program and/or country-wide after successful testing and modification. While such a process is complex and timing consuming, the potential payoffs in terms of efficiency gains are substantial.

VII. Delivery System Reforms

Jordan has a well-developed physical and human health infrastructure with substantial overall capacity, despite regional disparities in availability of services. The significant capital and manpower infrastructures of the major public programs overlap and are uncoordinated. There is little coordination with, and regulation of, the large and growing private sector (see Figure 7). Management information systems and computerization at all levels of the system are lacking. Management in the individual public programs is highly centralized, and there is virtually no overall policy coordination for the entire sector. The 63 percent occupancy rate is indicative of substantial excess capacity. The large number of referrals to hospitals and the overuse of hospital outpatient facilities relative to primary care clinics are indicative of the lack of an effective referral system as well as potential quality problems at the clinic level. The rapid growth of the largely unregulated private sector is indicative of access and quality problems in the public sector. The substantial excess capacity of the private sector, limited regulation of quality and price, and lack of relevant information on private sector utilization, capacity, and expenditures obviate the development of policies that maximize cost-effective use of total health resources. While Jordan has adequate numbers of physicians for its present and future needs, the quality of their educational preparation varies widely. Nurses are still in short supply. A reform strategy for improving the efficiency and effectiveness of the service delivery system must focus on management, manpower, and physical capital investment policies.

Management Reforms

Management reforms include overall management of the sector, and management of individual programs, facilities, and patients, as well as the development and availability of appropriate data for decision-making at all levels of the system. Jordan needs a permanent national level health policy coordinating body composed of representatives of all sectors and stakeholders (including consumers) with dedicated budget and staff. The Higher Health Council may have been established to perform that role, but has not for a variety of reasons, including turnover of key ministers, lack of specificity in its mandate, no formal meeting schedule, and lack of a dedicated budget and permanent staff. Either reform of the Higher Health Council or creation of a new such entity reporting to the Prime Minister, Crown Prince, and/or Council of Ministers is a *quid pro quo* for a coordinated and effective health policy process. A national level body that spans all programs and sectors is critical so that Jordan can effectively coordinate its public programs while at the same time harnessing the substantial capacity and high tech capabilities of the private sector in assuring access, equity, and efficient use of the total (public and private) resources devoted to health.

Management information systems are needed at every level of the system. Concomitantly, appropriate data for national level health policy decision-making are also needed. In particular, Jordan needs to develop national health accounts, information on the coverage status of the population by program, and information on private sector spending, utilization, capacity, health insurance, and self-insuring private firms as well. Decision-makers also need far more complete epidemiological information. On the service delivery side, Jordan needs a complete inventory of its major facilities in both public and private systems, as well as masterplans of those facilities.[55] Such information is needed for developing policies that effectively coordinate across the different public and private financing arrangements and delivery systems as well as for evaluating the impacts of policy changes financially, epidemiologically, and from a delivery system perspective.

Similarly, since the most effective resource allocation decisions are made by those closest to where the resources are actually utilized, the MOH should undertake a major decentralization effort. Such a reform effort would entail: streamlining the MOH and RMS bureaucracies and upgrading the management skills of top level MOH and local managers in decision-making, delegation, and monitoring. New management information systems would need to be put in place at ministry and individual facility levels. Reinstituting formal management training programs for both health program and facility managers at the university level would be an important first step. Such efforts are clearly necessary concomitants of the provider payment reforms discussed above.

Management of individual patients and more appropriate use of lower level facilities necessitates effective referral systems and some basic reforms including training in the primary care area. The types of reforms that should be considered include:

- Providing clinics with consistent inventories of drugs and supplies.
- Improve the scheduling of services in clinics through the introduction of an appointment system.
- Assigning hospital-based physicians (as in the RMS) to support and supervise free-standing clinics, including holding periodic specialty sessions at local clinic sites.
- For non-emergency care, requiring patients to have a written referral before the patient is accepted for care at hospital.
- Developing financial incentive systems for both patients (through additional user charges) and physicians (through provider payment reforms) to promote an effective referral system.

---

[55] MOH and RMS staff are currently preparing norms and standards for facilities and collecting relevant structural and operational data for development of a master plan for public facilities.

Manpower Reforms

In terms of health manpower, reforms dealing with the geographic distribution, training of physicians, nurses, and allied and technical personnel, and continuing education, could improve access, quality, and the efficiency of service delivery. While the current Health Management Project addresses some of these issues, further reforms are clearly warranted. There are regional disparities in the distribution of physicians as evidenced by a 3:1 difference in physician population ratios among Amman and some of the rural governorates. While the MOH has done a great deal to place clinics in these rural areas, it continuously faces the usual obstacles of placing professionals. Policies and appropriate incentives should be developed to attract and retain physicians in rural areas. In addition, the DALY analysis suggests the need to strengthen training, and increase the number of professionals trained, in emergency care and obstetric services.

Jordan needs to do more to strengthen and maintain the skills of all its health personnel, but especially nurses and other allied health and technical personnel. Foreign training is expensive and should focus more strongly on preparing qualified teachers, rather than practitioners, in the health disciplines. Medical curricula for undergraduates and postgraduates should be reformed from its current hospital orientation toward a community-based model emphasizing prevention and management of common childhood diseases and outpatient treatment and detection of chronic disorders such as diabetes and cancer. Certification procedures for physicians should be reviewed to ensure the quality of physician services. The nurse education system should be reviewed with the objective of perhaps consolidating the six different levels and streamlining the fragmented education path a nurse needs to follow in order to advance. Continuing education programs (such as conferences jointly sponsored by the MOH, RMS, JUH, and the private sector), need to be strengthened as well, making them more readily available to nurses, paramedical technicians, and other support staff.

Physical Infrastructure

Generally the physical condition of Jordan's health institutions is good, although there are problems in some facilities. Facilities are well constructed and installations and equipment are adequately specified and sufficient in number. However underlying this generally favorable overall picture of the physical structure of institutions are problems which include: inappropriate organization of rooms and equipment in relation to functional requirements, lack of an overview (particularly in the MOH) of the buildings, plant, estates, etc. which make up the health system infrastructure, regional disparities coupled with significant excess capacity overall resulting partially from lack of coordination among the multiple public and private financing and delivery systems, and inappropriate use of higher levels of the system due to poor referral networks. These problems result in inefficiency, diminished quality, limited access, and poor management.

With regard to individual facilities, while overall physical conditions are good, there are serious functional problems, especially in MOH facilities. Sites are often very overcrowded; departments are often not placed in correct functional proximity to each other; rooms are under-dimensioned and corridors and stairways are narrow and difficult to negotiate; and, important service rooms such as nurse stations, staff rooms, utility rooms, etc. are often missing. The JUH is slightly better, with conditions in RMS and private facilities being the best. A major reform is this area would be for the MOH, RMS, and JUH to develop appropriate norms and standards for (all) health facilities and their individual departments including standard schedules of accommodation, organizational diagrams, specifications and schedules of finishes, and equipment lists. The MOH, RMS, and JUH should also develop masterplans for each major existing and planned facility, and based on these masterplans undertake improvements in the functional conditions at these facilities.

In terms of overall system capacity, as discussed above, there is a surplus of beds, indicating that it should not be necessary to increase the beds in most institutions or governorates in the near future. For example, Jordan's current occupancy rate is 63 percent, well below a generally accepted norm of 80 percent.[56] With its current rate of population growth and current hospital utilization patterns, in theory Jordan would not have to add any new bed capacity until 2003. It would only need to make investments to replace existing obsolescent beds.[57] Figure 8 shows the total cost (capital and recurrent) on a year to year basis from 1996-2010 for two alternative policies: 1) building no new beds until the hospital occupancy rate reached 80 percent and increasing the number of beds thereafter with population growth to maintain an 80 percent occupancy level, and 2) continuing to increase the stock of hospital beds in proportion to future growth in population. The cumulative total costs of allowing beds to increase in proportion to population growth is US$274 million (JD 196 million), while the total cost of the 80 percent occupancy policy is US$136 million (JD 97 million). In other words, if Jordan were to follow a future investment strategy based on an 80 percent occupancy level instead of its growth in population, its cumulative hospital investment expenditures over the next 15 years would be halved.

---

[56] An occupancy rate of 80 percent is a frequently applied benchmark. Defining the optimal occupancy rate depends on the demographic and epidemiological characteristics of the population, the range of hospital services available, and the willingness to tolerate queues and/or shortages of services at certain times.

[57] In practice, this would be a challenging policy to implement, given the current difference between the occupancy rates in the public and private sectors (69 percent versus 49 percent), and the need to both meet social needs and support private sector economic development.

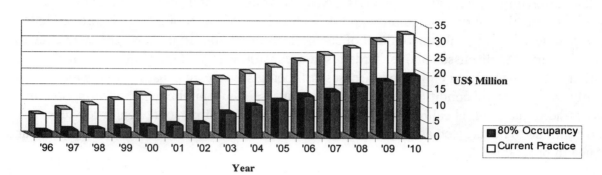

**Figure 8. Hospital Capital and Recurrent Expenditures
Under Alternative Investment Strategies**

Source: M. Hopkinson, "Health Sector Study Mission: Buildings and Equipment," Report from the November 1995
Mission to Jordan, World Bank, Washington, D.C., January 1996.

However, there are serious geographic disparities as demonstrated by a 3:1 difference in beds per capita between Amman and some rural governorates. Clearly any future investment strategy for replacing obsolescent beds and building new ones must address this issue, as well as the differential excess capacity levels in the public and private sectors. In fact, an appropriate investment strategy would flow from the development of the proposed masterplan discussed above. Concomitantly, an investment strategy should be based on better coordination among public facilities as well as the private sector. Such coordination should flow both from the management improvements suggested above as well as the proposed provider payment reforms. Similarly, more appropriate use of facilities is contingent upon an effective referral system.

In summary, while improvements in management and provider payment would alleviate some of the basic efficiency, access, and quality problems inherent in the current physical infrastructure, other reform measures should also be undertaken. These include:

- Developing appropriate norms and standards for health facilities
- Developing masterplans for all major secondary and tertiary facilities
- Improving the functional conditions at MOH, RMS and JUH facilities
- Formulating an investment strategy based on need that is targeted at removing regional disparities

VIII. *Reform of Health Programs and Clinical Practice*

Reforming health programs which are targeted at the major causes of death and disability, as well as behavioral (e.g., nutrition, exercise, wearing seatbelts) and environmental factors, have the greatest potential for directly improving the health status of the population. Improvements in clinical practice are a logical concomitant of such efforts and will also improve the efficiency of service delivery. As discussed above, Jordan is at a transition stage in its epidemiological transition with maternal and childhood diseases still being significant causes of death and disability, while chronic conditions are the leading causes. Thus, public health efforts, both in terms of traditional public health activities and public financing of personal health services, should continue to be targeted at specific maternal and childhood problems as well as particular adult health programs.

Given limited resources, the most economically efficient way to reduce the disease burden is by supporting programs that provide the largest reduction in disability and death per dinar spent, or alternatively have the lowest cost per DALY saved. Figure 9 provides information on the cost-effectiveness of different interventions on the basis of the cost per DALY gained using Jordanian cost information.[58] There are 10-70 fold variations in the cost-effectiveness of different interventions, ranging from US$150 per DALY gained from TB treatment to US$10,500 per DALY gained for coronary artery by-pass surgery. Rational public health investment policy necessitates considering at least three factors: burden of the disease, cost-effectiveness of treatment, and, for infectious diseases, the future potential DALY loss of non-intervention. For example, as shown in Figure 9, TB does not now result in a major DALY loss; however, if TB is not controlled it will result in a serious DALY loss in the future due to its infectious nature.[59] Conversely, coronary artery bypass surgery is targeted to treating ischemic heart disease which causes the largest DALY loss, but it is not a cost-effective treatment. This in turn necessitates considering cost-effective preventive interventions such as anti-smoking campaigns which would address in part the disease burden from ischemic heart disease (cigarette smoking is linked to 20 percent of the DALY loss in Table 3).

---

[58] See Cowley and Claeson, op. cit.

[59] This is part of the reason the cost of the intervention per DALY saved is so low. There is an effective and relatively inexpensive intervention, and it will prevent a great deal of future DALY loss.

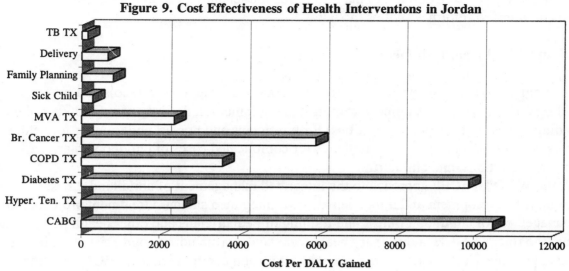

Figure 9. Cost Effectiveness of Health Interventions in Jordan

Notes: "TX" = Treatment
            "MVA" = Motor Vehicle Accidents
            "COPD" = Chronic Obstructive Pulmonary Disease
            "CABG" = Cardiac Bypass Surgery
Source: P. Cowley and M. Claeson, "Public Health Interventions and Cost Effectiveness,"
            Report from the November 1995 Mission to Jordan, World Bank, Washington, D.C., 1996.

Given Jordan's epidemiological and medical treatment cost structures, the burden of disease/cost-effectiveness analysis leads to three broad conclusions:

• There are cost-effective interventions in both the maternal and child health areas to reduce the still significant disease burden of these populations.

• With regard to adult health, certain tertiary based care interventions, such as cardiac bypass surgery, are not cost-effective, although they do address diseases causing a significant part of Jordan's burden of illness.

• Certain moderately cost-effective interventions (i.e., hypertension management) targeted at 'high burden' chronic conditions, could become more cost-effective by improving efficiency in the delivery system (e.g., more outpatient prevention, detection, and treatment) and through reforms in the pharmaceutical sector (e.g., treatment protocols for first line anti-diabetic drugs).

Reforms in health programs and clinical practice span a wide range of activities including development of treatment protocols, improvements in the delivery of care (including family planning services), training of medical practitioners, and health promotion including extensive consumer education. The reforms in the adult and child health areas could lead to significant reductions in Jordan's burden of illness and improve overall health status. A number of areas that have not been addressed by this study that have important implications for health are the areas of food and water safety, sanitation, transport safety, substance abuse, dental health, geriatric care, and environmental/occupational health. A separate study focusing on these areas would be an appropriate concomitant to the reform recommendations enumerated below. Specific recommended reform activities include:

Maternal and Child Health Reforms

- Improve antenatal and delivery services through standard treatment protocols and by providing ongoing advanced clinical training and equipment in delivery care (including the upgrading of cesarean section capabilities) for physicians and nurses, and training for health workers in the appropriate referral strategies for complicated cases of childhood diarrhea, respiratory infections, and childbirth.
- Adapt the WHO/UNICEF approach to the integrated management of childhood illness including the development and implementation of integrated standard treatment protocols for the management of childhood illness and training of pediatricians and other health personnel.
- Expand the roles of MCH and primary health care centers (including appropriate training) to provide community outreach information, education, and communication (IEC) programs, including informal group meetings on maternal and child health issues.
- Focus on eliminating the large regional disparities in mother and child health outcomes.
- Improve family planning services by: (i) increasing the availability and variety of modern contraceptives; (ii) integrating family planning into maternal and child health care; (iii) strengthening IEC campaigns that address family planning; (iv) providing targeted training to health care providers; (v) ensuring that adequate privacy is available in health facilities to discuss family planning options; and (vi) better coordinating the activities of the various players in the sector (including NGOs, donors, the Government, and the private sector).

Adult Health Reforms

- Develop treatment protocols for outpatient-based diagnosis and treatment of important chronic diseases such as hypertension, diabetes, and chronic obstructive pulmonary disease.
- Promote outpatient treatment of chronic conditions by having hospital-based endocrinologists, pulmonologists, obstetricians, and cardiologists periodically visit comprehensive health centers to render clinical services and train staff in the prevention and management of chronic illnesses.
- Undertake a major patient education effort in anti-smoking, exercise, and nutrition and establish patient education centers for chronic disorders.
- Develop a comprehensive national cancer control strategy which includes expansions of anti-smoking campaigns and early detection of cancer (particularly breast cancer).
- Develop a national road safety program including penalties for non-use of seat belts.
- Provide training and education to physicians to promote the rational use of drugs.
- Collect information on the incidence and risk factors associated with adult mortality and morbidity, and undertake behavioral research on effective health promotion mechanisms.

IX. *Pharmaceutical Sector Reforms*

The consumption and production of pharmaceuticals are important components of Jordan's health spending as well as industrial structure and export base. Pharmaceutical expenditures through both public and private sectors accounted for 27 percent of total health expenditures, JD 88 million, and two percent of GDP. Jordan has eight pharmaceutical factories with five more under construction producing JD 79 million of products annually, three quarters of which are exported (accounting for some four percent of total goods exports). While most pharmaceuticals are readily available and there are few quality problems,[60] there are a number of significant problems with their procurement, management, dispensing, pricing, and consumption. These include:

- Lack of a national drug policy
- Lack of an essential drug list for the public sector
- Inefficiencies in the management and regulatory system
- Weaknesses and redundancies in the distribution and storage systems
- Inefficient pharmaceutical pricing policies
- Inefficient prescribing and consumption practices

There is no overall national drug policy. The pharmaceutical sector is guided by the 1972 Practicing of Pharmacy Law, its various amendments, past practices, and MOH directives. This body of law and regulations deals mainly with the role of the retail pharmacist and to a much lesser degree with the role of importers, wholesalers, and the manufacturing sector. The 'law' does not address such critical issues as Good Manufacturing Practices, WHO's Certificate on Pharmaceutical Produce, intellectual property rights, and the role of generic drugs, including generic substitution. The lack of a comprehensive modern policy framework is an obstacle to better management and development of the sector. The lack of an essential drug list in the public sector and a similar list of essential drugs for insurance reimbursement schemes reduces the possibility of both procurement and insurance systems to give priority to vital and essential drugs.

The time consuming and cumbersome processes to register drugs, along with the pricing system discussed below, are barriers to the use of low cost commodity generics. Indeed, it is unlikely that a commodity generic manufacturer will register his drugs, since the possibility of a successful marketing is quite small given the long registration process, the relatively small size of the market, the pricing system, and prevailing prescribing practices in Jordan. Jordan may want to consider using a "shared registration system" or accepting documentation and approval from highly developed drug authorities in other countries for registration purposes.

---

[60] While quality control is generally good, and there are few problems with smuggled, illicit, fake, and spurious drugs, further improvements in quality could be achieved through technological improvements in the quality control laboratory and upgrading the skills of drug inspectors.

The MOH, RMS, JUH, UNRWA, and the private sector all have separate pharmaceutical procurement, storage, distribution, and policies on the use of drugs. There is limited collaboration among systems. Each sector forecasts its demand based on their best estimates of past consumption, availability of funds and anticipated demand. This does not provide an approximation of the 'medical needs' of the country since it is not based on underlying treatment episodes and standard treatment schedules. There clearly could be significant saving from both upgrading storage techniques (e.g., inventory and management control) and combining some of these functions among programs. While the procurement procedures used by the public programs result in the purchase of drugs at internationally competitive prices, the private sector procurement prices are well above such levels (perhaps on the order of 30 percent above the retail prices in advanced markets). A joint agency for coordination and procurement of drugs, medical consumables, and technology with updated drug information and prices, sources of prices of materials, performance of suppliers, etc. would facilitate procurement planning and might well reduce costs.

There is significant overuse of expensive drugs due to the absence of an essential drug list, generous coverage policies of public programs, lack of generic prescribing or substitution, lack of pharmaceutical treatment protocols for physicians, and the regulatory pricing practices in the private sector. Individuals covered by the MOH and RMS face trivial cost-sharing for drugs prescribed by public providers even when these drugs are purchased through the private sector. Without a list of priority drugs, doctors will tend to prescribe the newest, often most heavily promoted and expensive drugs, even when the therapeutic advantage is minimal. Patients will often want the latest and most expensive drugs, particularly when the costs are heavily subsidized. With virtually no cost-consciousness on the part of the consumer or physician, there are no real incentives for the rational use of drugs. Inappropriate use is further encouraged by the lack of standard treatment schedules (e.g., guidelines for rational use of antibiotics for treatment of dysentery, ARI, diabetes, and most other common conditions). There is also very little use of generics. Physicians prescribe brand name drugs for the most part, and generic substitution is not allowed. Allowance for generic substitution would provide many patients with lower priced, but bio-equivalent branded or commodity generics. Improvements in the rational use of drugs should be planned following a review of the current training in pharmacology and therapeutics, the availability of continuing education, and the integration of the experiences of doctors trained abroad.

The fixed percentage markup pricing policies (21.5 percent) for private sector drugs encourage pharmacies to sell the most expensive brand name drugs. Ironically, this policy may be disadvantaging Jordan's pharmaceutical exporters. Domestic products are generally priced below similar drugs in industrialized countries, and the 21.5 percent mark-up is small by international standards. Most importing countries have pricing policies which correlate what they will pay to the price in the exporting countries domestic market. Many exporting countries attempt to favor their drug export industry by allowing high prices in the local market and then use reimbursements to reduce the price to the patients. Jordan may wish to consider this element if it decides to overhaul its present pricing system.

Reforms of the pharmaceutical sector could lead to significant savings, better quality and improved health outcomes. A modern, comprehensive drug policy may facilitate investments in the industry and pave the way for improved management and use of drugs. It will also simplify MOH's administration of the drug sector. Based on this review and experience from comparable countries, it might be possible to reduce the overall annual drug bill by 20-40 percent. The largest initial savings would come from the introduction of generic substitution at the retail level. In the long-run savings would accrue from more coordinated forecasting of demand, and more efficient procurement, storage, and distribution. The use of a national essential drug list, limitations on the number of drugs being reimbursed, increased cost sharing, standard treatment schedules, and training in the rational use of drugs will result in both savings and therapeutic advantages.

Reforms should be targeted at all stakeholders and include:

- Developing and implementing a national drug policy and a modern pharmaceutical law
- Establishing a national list of essential drugs
- Overhauling the present pricing system
- Introducing computer-assisted methods of forecasting annual drug requirements based on morbidity and service statistics
- Establishing a joint agency for the procurement of drugs, consumables, and medical technology
- Implementing computerized methods of inventory control and exploring the feasibility of manufacturers delivering to health facilities directly
- Exploring potential economies from combining storage and distribution networks
- Developing treatment standards, their introduction, and training in the rational use of drugs (e.g., generic substitution)
- Undertaking training in drug management, rational prescribing, and public education in the use of drugs

Given the size of the sector, its complexity and numerous different areas that need to be addressed in depth, the appropriate way to proceed would be to undertake a study of these various proposed reform areas. Problems should be analyzed in detail. Proposed solutions should be developed based on local conditions as well as international experience. All this needs to be done in the context of an overall sector strategy that coordinates reforms across the separate public and private programs and the domestic pharmaceutical industry.

X. A Proposed Health Reform Process

Jordan's health system performs well in terms of access and health outcomes. Yet, the system is expensive and inequitable, and quality can be variable. Rapid growth of the largely unregulated private sector in an era of constrained public spending is resulting in a two tiered system of care. Lack of a coordinated policy apparatus and relevant data for decision-making preclude effective policy-making across Jordan's multiple financing arrangements and delivery systems. With private financing accounting for over 50 percent of all health spending and private delivery capacity providing more than 30 percent of overall delivery system capacity and growing, Jordan has come to a crossroads. Passive acceptance of the status quo will result in a U.S. type system with costs out of control, gaps in coverage and access problems for vulnerable populations, wasteful excess capacity, and relatively poor health outcomes for the amounts spent. Moreover, the continued costs of the public programs driven by the epidemiological transition, population aging, a continued high birth rate, and clinical and economic inefficiencies will hinder efforts to achieve macroeconomic stability and growth.

Implementing a major reform agenda is replete with difficulties, both economic and political. All reforms have winners and losers. Those stakeholders who have the most to lose, generally certain medical care provider groups, pharmaceutical suppliers, and other powerful groups in the medical industrial complex, will likely oppose reforms. Those who would gain (e.g., the uncovered population) are generally the least vocal. Given the political sensitivity of health reforms, it is important to have a transparent process, strong support from top political leadership, and involve all stakeholders. If important players are left out of the debate, they are likely to sabotage the development of reforms and their implementation. The policy process is at least as important as the substance of the reforms themselves.

A necessary condition for an effective and sustainable health reform process in Jordan is the establishment of a permanent national level body composed of representatives of all public and private sector programs and other relevant stakeholders, including consumers. Such a body needs dedicated staff, policy analytic capacity, and an earmarked budget. It should meet regularly and have the ability to interact and contract with relevant public and private insurers, providers, consumers, academics, NGOs, international organizations, bilateral assistance agencies, and other relevant governmental and non-governmental organizations.

This national level body should have a broad mandate and the authority to deal with the following types of generic reform areas:

- Health policy process and data for decision-making
- Socioeconomic/epidemiological status of the population, population growth and distribution, and underlying health needs
- Total health system costs (present and future) and how they are financed
- Universal coverage and the present gaps
- The configuration of the service delivery system including geographic maldistribution
- Medical care provider payment

- Health manpower and training
- Clinical practice
- Public health
- Individual responsibility
- Pharmaceutical sector
- Public sector coordination, fiscal federalism (i.e., the relationship between the central and regional governments) and decentralization
- The institutional structure and regulation of the private sector including insurance regulation

A proposal to establish such a body by reconstituting a modified version of Jordan's Higher Health Council has been submitted to the Government and could form the base for a coordinated major health reform effort. Once established, the Council will need to prioritize its activities. It will need to choose among competing reform priorities. Some of the reform activities recommended in this study, such as developing management information systems and norms for public facilities, have already been initiated. Others, such as medical care provider payment reforms, will need to be undertaken over a more medium term focus. Management issues including obtaining relevant data for decision-making should be given a high priority since such information is crucial for effective policy-making. For example, better coordination between public and private sectors can only occur if there is more transparency regarding the private delivery system and private health insurance, and relevant information about private health insurance, private sector capacity, utilization, and costs is available. Health sector reform priorities will also have to be carefully reconciled with budget priorities as the costs of different reforms will have to be weighed against their benefits in terms of improvements in health outcomes, efficiency, equity, quality, and consumer satisfaction as well as alternative non-health investments.

Reform Agenda

This study has identified information and analysis gaps that need to be addressed as part of the reform process. Given the timing, political and organizational complexities in initiating a major public reform process, moving ahead in the areas recommended by this study will provide much of the underlying informational and analytical base for such a broad reform effort. This study has identified several areas of needed reforms dealing with more effective management, improved access, a more efficient service delivery system, improving health status and clinical practice, and improving efficiency, quality, and management of the pharmaceutical sector. Efforts could be initiated to provide basic information and analysis in each of these areas to inform the reform process. Possible activities in these areas would include:

(i)   Improve management of the health sector by:

- Improving management capacity at every level of the system including providing management information systems, computerization, and training.

- Developing necessary data for decision-making including National Health Accounts, coverage information, basic epidemiological information on mortality, morbidity, and underlying risk factors, and basic cost information at the individual facility level.

- Decentralizing decision-making to the facility level, and providing individual facility managers with the necessary authority and management information to effectively manage their facilities.

(ii)   Improve health status and clinical practice by:

- Developing and disseminating treatment protocols for communicable and non-communicable diseases and providing appropriate training in their use.

- Adapting the WHO/UNICEF approach to integrated management of childhood illness.

- Focusing programs to eliminate regional disparities in maternal and child health outcomes.

- Improving the availability and delivery of family planning services.

- Promoting outpatient treatment of chronic conditions.

- Undertaking a major health education effort in anti-smoking, exercise, nutrition, and the wearing of seat belts.

- Developing a comprehensive national cancer control strategy which includes expansions of anti-smoking programs and early detection of cancer (particularly breast cancer).

(iii)   Improve equity and access by extending formal universal coverage to the entire population by:

- Undertaking a major study that analyzes the costs, alternative financing arrangements, and implementation issues associated with a politically acceptable set of options.

- Including universal coverage as the centerpiece in a major national reform effort.

(iv)   Improve the efficiency and clinical effectiveness of the service delivery system by:

- Developing options to reform Jordan's centralized medical care provider payment systems.

- Developing appropriate norms and standards for facilities.

- Undertaking a comprehensive study to establish an effective referral system for the individual public programs as well as across programs focusing on needed training, patient and physician incentives, scheduling, and improvements in physical infrastructure, supplies, and equipment.

- Developing a masterplan of all major secondary and tertiary facilities in the MOH, RMS, and JUH and ultimately in the private sector.

- Developing a capital investment strategy to eliminate excess capacity, redress geographic imbalances in service availability, and improve the functional conditions in MOH, RMS and JUH facilities.

(v)   Improve efficiency, health outcomes, and quality of the pharmaceutical sector by undertaking a major study and reform focusing on:

- Developing a national pharmaceutical policy including a list of essential drugs for public programs and overhaul of the present pricing system.

- Analyzing the potential economies from combining some or all the procurement, storage, and distribution functions of the five separate systems.

- Introducing advanced methods of forecasting annual drug requirements based on morbidity and service use statistics.

- Developing and introducing standard treatment protocols, and training in the rational use of drugs (standard treatment schedules, generic substitution).

A Health Reform Process

Once a permanent national body has been established, staffed, and funded, one possible road map to major national reform would be the following approach:

- Obtain input from all relevant stakeholders through public forums, hearings, solicitation of written comments, and discussions of the issues in the media. The joint Jordanian/World Bank Health Sector Study could be presented and discussed in a public forum to facilitate the debate.

- Task force staff should develop recommendations for reform based on the strengths and weaknesses of the present system, the analyses recommended above, input from the public forums, and real world political, economic, and institutional constraints. Separate subgroups may need to be created to deal with different issues.

- Reform recommendations should be developed, 'costed out', and thoroughly analyzed in the context of overall reform goals and institutional realities.

- Submit the reform recommendations to the political process, possibly undertaking demonstration projects and evaluations of individual reforms in particular institutions and/or geographic areas.

- Implement the reform agenda with sufficient up-front timing to put the necessary infrastructure in place for the reforms to succeed. There should also be a process to evaluate the reforms so that necessary mid-course corrections can be made.

Strong leadership, dedicated staff, strong multi-disciplinary analytical capacity, and effective public relations capabilities are a sine qua non for the success of such an effort. Health care financing and delivery systems are highly country-specific socioeconomic organisms, which affect all aspects of a country's development and touch important political constituencies. Jordanian reformers will have to deal with all these elements.

ANNEX 1

HEALTH FINANCING MODEL FOR JORDAN

I.   Specification of Public and Private Financing Options

Developing, evaluating and implementing universal coverage policies is a complex and highly political undertaking with major economic implications. For this study, a financial impact model to assess such economic inputs was developed and used to analyze two universal coverage options for Jordan in order to illustrate the types of issues and analyses that would need to be addressed should the Government of Jordan (GOJ) decide to proceed with a major reform effort in this area.

Universal coverage could be implemented in Jordan through a variety of methods. Options would include:

- formalizing universal coverage by expanding the Civil Insurance Program
- expanding coverage through the Social Security Corporation
- implementing other employer mandates or other national approaches (for example, sickness fund and general revenue financed systems)

Civil Insurance Option. For persons with government insurance, the services received in government facilities are provided at very low consumer cost. Even for persons without insurance, services provided in MOH facilities are heavily subsidized, since the prices charged cover only a small fraction of the cost of services. Given this starting point, which is close to universal coverage with some consumer cost-sharing, one straightforward option would be to expand the Civil Insurance Program. All persons without other insurance coverage could be required to buy insurance through this program, adding costs for additional hospital services and lowered cost-sharing, but generating some offsetting revenues from premiums.

Social Security Option. Use of the Social Security Corporation to provide health insurance to persons associated with covered workers would be consistent with Jordan's original Social Security Act. The section of the act authorizing such coverage, however, has never been implemented. Implementing this section in conjunction with MOH coverage of those not subject to Social Security would be a plausible means of providing universal coverage.

Other Options. As an alternative to government provision of health care, employer mandates would allow coverage of most of the population with health insurance of whatever depth and breadth is desired, presumably in conjunction with a limited government residual program. Beyond the direct mandate (leaving details to the employers), use of quasi-governmental insuring entities would also fit this approach.

II. Simulate Impacts on Costs, Utilization, and Financing Sources

Definitions of Cost

Consideration of universal health care options will be greatly affected by the estimated costs of each option. From a policy perspective, there are three basic types of cost which are examined. The first is "program cost", defined as the total expenditures of the insuring agency (new or existing) attributable to the new program. This is the cost which is of special concern to government agencies which are quantifying the budget changes required. The second, and usually most important, is the "net government cost". This cost represents the change in total government spending after the new program is implemented, the key cost concept when government spending levels overall are an area of special political sensitivity. The third is "society cost", which quantifies the change in total spending for medical care, irrespective of who pays for it. This change in spending reflects induced demand, payment level changes and efficiency changes. Induced demand is the change in consumption (both utilization and quality) produced by changes in prices and access from a system change. Payment level changes reflect changes in fee schedules within an existing system as well as the creation of new payment systems. Efficiency changes can be either improved or reduced efficiency.

The basic modeling approach used here is based on the use of National Health Accounts (NHA). The approach can be viewed as a supplement to the current methods used by the various GOJ entities which have been analyzing reform options. Use of NHA as a starting point provides a framework for integrating data and assumptions consistently. This allows the analyst to watch the whole system while modeling the impact of reform and make explicit adjustments for any factors needed. The emphasis is on use of the best available data, even when the data are not good. The consistent starting point facilitates making quick estimates, which can be improved later if interest in the policy option remains. The process separates arguments over baselines from arguments over policy effects (although it does not eliminate either). The approach can be employed with paper and pencil, spreadsheets, or high-level computer languages.

Basic Methodology

Step 1: Development of NHA

NHA are a matrix of sources of funds by type of service which summarize total health expenditures. Sources of funds reflect the entities paying for services, for example, government agencies, consumers out-of-pocket spending, private insurers, workers compensation. Types of service are the different forms of medical care consumed such as hospital services, clinics, physician contacts, pharmaceuticals, dental care, etc.

The details which need to be estimated in each dimension depend on how the health care system works currently and how it will work under reform. Service splits are needed for services which have their own financing (cost-sharing, reimbursement system, etc.), or which have different behavioral responses expected under reform. Source of funds, at a minimum, separate out out-of-pocket payments, private insurance, and government agency payments. Normally, each agency's payments would be a distinct source. Out-of-pocket payments may also distinguish between cost-sharing associated with insured patients and direct patient payments for uninsured services.

Once the overall NHA has been developed, additional matrices will be created which partition the national totals into sub-accounts for population subgroups. Subgroups would be created based on dimensions such as primary source of insurance, income class, geographic location, age, and employment status.

Also associated with the NHA and the matrices for subgroups could be auxiliary matrices breaking out utilization of services. While expenditures are the main focus of the model, consumption of medical services is frequently important to policymakers in evaluating alternative options. Other auxiliary matrices could include data on income sources associated with specific sources of funds (for example, distinguishing premium income from general revenues for government provided services), and splits by ownership of provider for type of service (for example, distinguishing spending in privately owned hospitals versus government owned facilities).

In general, the NHA is developed for the most recent year for which data are reasonably complete. For example, during calendar year 1995, the base year for NHA development would probably be 1994, at best. Even then, some data is likely to be unavailable for 1994, and will have to be projected from earlier years. Once the base year NHA is developed, then it is projected to the current year and then to future years as needed. For example, since a universal coverage option could take several years to implement, projecting the NHA to 1997 would be required.

Step 2: Calculate Transfers

Once the NHA is developed for the years to be analyzed, the next step is to trim the NHA down to a Covered Services Matrix (CSM). This requires making two sets of adjustments to the total matrix. First, programs which are outside the scope of the reform proposals are excluded. For example, public health activities may be in the budget of agencies which also provide personal health care. Such services would normally be outside the scope of any universal health care reform, and should be subtracted out of the CSM. Second, one has to exclude items of personal health care which are for services not covered by reforms, e.g., cosmetic surgery and experimental procedures. If the NHA itself had already been split by population subgroup, then the CSM adjustments would be repeated at the subgroup level.

Once the CSM is completed, the task of estimating the shifts of spending from existing sources of funds to the new program can be executed. Frequently this proceeds simultaneously with a re-examination of the specifications of the proposed plan, since ambiguities in the proposal often only become apparent when attempts are being made to determine how a particular set of people are affected by the reform. In general terms, the calculations associated with the Transfers Step involve moving the covered charges associated with the new program down to that line of the CSM (a line of zeroes under current law), and then pulling the cost-sharing back out and putting it in the out-of-pocket line. In some cases, the proposal rearranges responsibilities for some groups within existing programs, so the transfers will be among line items for those programs, rather than involving a new line item.

Step 3: Calculate Future Law Profile

Once the effect of the reform proposal in terms of how existing spending will flow has been estimated, the impact of the reform on the level of spending itself must be estimated. The three principal impacts to consider here are induction, payment rates, and efficiency.

The "induction impact" of a reform is the change in spending caused by a change in the out-of-pocket expenses associated with receiving services. For example, persons without insurance who receive care in MOH facilities pay specified amounts for pharmaceuticals, and other services. Moving these populations to an insured status would greatly reduce the out-of-pocket obligations associated with each unit of service. Depending on the assumed price elasticity of demand for each type of medical service, there would be varying increases in the demand for each of those forms of care.

The second set of adjustments to be made involves changes in "payment rates". Reform proposals often involve shifting services among providers who have different price levels. For example, requiring employers to purchase health insurance for employees could shift services from MOH facilities to private facilities, if the insurance made even partial payments toward private care. In that case, the Transfer Step would have shown a shift of spending from MOH to private facilities, but the spending would still have reflected MOH cost levels. The Future Law Profile Step would then be the point at which those expenditures would be adjusted for the higher private facility prices.

A third set of adjustments to be made requires consideration of changes in the "efficiency" of various sets of providers as a result of the reforms. For example, a reform which shifts services from overcrowded facilities to under-utilized facilities may raise efficiency, so the total spending associated with the Transfer Step analysis would have to be reduced in the Future Law Profile step.

III. Analysis of Impacts

Universal Coverage through Expansion of the Civil Insurance Program

The basic approach would involve issuing insurance cards to all persons without access to other formal coverage. It is assumed that cost-sharing rates and premiums would be similar to that incurred by civilian government employees under the existing programs.

The NHA shown in Exhibit 1 is a simplified partitioning of total health spending for 1994, using government statistics for government program outlays and assuming private spending as a percent of GDP is comparable to 1988 levels, projected to 1994. A more complete explanation of the development of the totals by payer is provided in Attachment 1. The outlays from government programs were adjusted for payments from one entity to another (deleting double counting), and payments from consumers to government were shown as out-of-pocket spending if they were for cost-sharing but were left in the government program receiving the funds if they were premiums. The splits by service reflect the estimates shown in the University of Jordan study "Application of Health Insurance Schemes for Participants in the Social Security System" completed for the Social Security Corporation in 1994.

Exhibit 1. Jordan National Health Accounts (1994) (JD Million)					
	Type of Service				
Source of funds	*Total*	Inpatient Hospital	Ambulatory Care	Drugs	Other
Total	332.0	119.9	90.7	88.2	33.2
Out-of-pocket	140.0	48.9	36.9	54.2	0.0
MOH	84.8	21.4	16.2	14.0	33.2
RMS	34.1	22.9	5.2	6.0	0.0
Other public	10.0	3.4	2.6	4.0	0.0
Other private	63.1	23.3	29.8	10.0	0.0

Notes: *Service splits are based on Jordan University, "Applications of Health Insurance Schemes for Participation in the Social Security System," 1994. Source of funds splits are based on official expenditure levels for government programs, and estimated insurance, cost sharing, and direct payment rates for private expenses.*
Source: James Mays and Vivian Hon, World Bank, 1996.

The development of the CSM in the Transfers Step reflects only one adjustment - deletion of the "public health" component. The assumption of 10 percent of total national spending falling into that category could be improved by a line-item analysis of the MOH budget (the assumed source of all such spending).

At this point, the CSM is also broken by population group. For this simplified example, the only split made is by primary insurance, and there the split is only between those with formal coverage versus those without. The major assumptions required to make this split are the fractions of persons without formal coverage and their relative spending level compared to those with formal coverage (see Attachment 2).

		Exhibit 2. *Covered Service Matrix* (JD Million) Population Group: No Formal Insurance			
		Type of Service			
Source of funds	*Total*	Inpatient Hospital	Ambulatory Care	Drugs	Other
Total	43.0	18.0	13.6	11.4	0.0
Out-of-pocket	21.5	6.0	4.1	11.4	0.0
MOH	21.5	12.0	9.5	0.0	0.0
RMS	0.0	0.0	0.0	0.0	0.0
Other public	0.0	0.0	0.0	0.0	0.0
Other private	0.0	0.0	0.0	0.0	0.0

Source: James Mays and Vivian Hon, World Bank, 1996.

Exhibit 2 shows the CSM for the set of persons lacking formal insurance coverage. This is based on 20 percent of the population being without formal coverage. (Alternative assumptions of 15 percent and 25 percent are discussed below.) The uninsured population is assumed to have lower per capita costs than the population as a whole. Since this subgroup is expected to have lower incomes on average, a 10 percent reduction in the expected price level of providers used is embedded in the estimate. Secondly, since the subgroup by definition is paying out-of-pocket for services (beyond the subsidies implied by the MOH serving as provider of last resort), a 20 percent reduction is made in the expected utilization rates. Thus, the total spending for covered services for the uninsured population is calculated as total spending (JD 332 million) minus uncovered services (JD 33.2 million) times the fraction of the people uninsured (0.20) times the relative provider price level for these people (1-0.10) times the relative utilization for these people (1-0.20):

$$(332.0 - 33.2) \times 0.20 \times (1-0.10) \times (1-0.20) = \text{JD 43.0 million.}$$

The main effect of this proposal would be to move expenditures for persons with no formal insurance from out-of-pocket to MOH. Exhibit 3 shows the effect of the transfer calculations on the CSM for this subgroup. (The proposal should have negligible effects on other groups). While most spending is shown moving to MOH, a small amount remains in out-of-pocket. This reflects the small cost-sharing requirements.

		Type of Service			
Source of funds	*Total*	Inpatient Hospital	Ambulatory Care	Drugs	Other
Total	43.0	18.0	13.6	11.4	0.0
Out-of-pocket	4.5	1.3	3.0	0.2	0.0
MOH	38.6	16.7	10.6	11.2	0.0
RMS	0.0	0.0	0.0	0.0	0.0
Other public	0.0	0.0	0.0	0.0	0.0
Other private	0.0	0.0	0.0	0.0	0.0

Exhibit 3. Transfers Matrix
(JD Million)
Population Group: No Formal Insurance

Source: James Mays and Vivian Hon, World Bank, 1996.

In generating the Future Law Profile, the only adjustment to make here is induction. The proposal should have minimal impacts on payment rates, and efficiency changes are not obviously generated. There are numerous ways to estimate the induction effect of changing out-of-pocket costs. One relatively simple method is called "uniform induction". With this method, the change in spending is calculated as a factor (called the induction parameter, denoted IP) times the change in out-of-pocket spending.

new spending = old spending + (IP x change in out-of-pocket spending)

For the population lacking formal insurance, the change in out-of-pocket leads to additional spending. Exhibit 4 shows total spending by this population rises moderately, about JD 13 million in 1994 terms. Spending by the government would rise about JD 30 million. Induction parameters for each type of service are shown. Total increases in spending are at the bottom of the table.

Exhibit 4. Future Law Profile Matrix (1994) (JD Million) Population Group: No Formal Insurance					
Type of Service					
Source of funds	*Total*	Inpatient Hospital	Ambulatory Care	Drugs	Other
Total	56.4	19.4	14.4	22.6	0.0
Out-of-pocket	5.0	1.4	3.2	0.5	0.0
MOH	51.5	18.1	11.2	22.2	0.0
RMS	0.0	0.0	0.0	0.0	0.0
Other public	0.0	0.0	0.0	0.0	0.0
Other private	0.0	0.0	0.0	0.0	0.0
Induction Parameter [1]		0.3	0.7	1.0	
Increase	13.4	1.4	0.8	11.2	-

Notes: [1] *American Academy of Actuaries, "Medical Savings Accounts: Cost Implications and Design Issues," p.4.*
Source: James Mays and Vivian Hon, World Bank, 1996.

For example, inpatient hospital spending by the uninsured is estimated to be JD 18 million (Exhibit 2), of which JD 6 million are out-of-pocket expenses (some daily charges for MOH facilities, the rest representing full costs for use of private facilities). With universal coverage, the Transfers Matrix (Exhibit 3) shows that the out-of-pocket spending would be reduced to JD 1.3 million, with the MOH becoming responsible for the rest. This decline in out-of-pocket spending of JD 4.7 million should lead to higher utilization of hospital services. The induction parameter (IP) for hospital services assumed here is 0.3. Thus, the JD 4.7 million reduction in out-of-pocket spending would lead to a JD 1.4 million increase in total consumption of hospital services (4.7 million times 0.3). These new expenditures in turn are allocated across the out-of-pocket and MOH sources of funds lines in the Future Law Profile Matrix (Exhibit 4).

Adding back the rest of the population gives the total Future Law Profile shown in Exhibit 5.

Exhibit 5. Future Law Profile Matrix (1994) (JD Million) Population Group: Total					
		Type of Service			
Source of funds	*Total*	In-patient Hospital	Ambulatory Care	Drugs	Other
Total	345.4	121.3	91.4	99.4	33.2
Out-of- pocket	123.4	44.2	36.0	43.2	0.0
MOH	114.8	27.5	17.9	36.2	33.2
RMS	34.1	22.9	5.2	6.0	0.0
Other public	10.0	3.4	2.6	4.0	0.0
Other private	63.1	23.3	29.8	10.0	0.0

Source: James Mays and Vivian Hon, World Bank, 1996.

Total program cost would be about JD 52 million. The JD 30 million increase in government outlays would be buying additional services (especially pharmaceuticals) for the newly covered population. The outlay increase could be partially offset through premium collections from the newly covered. If each family head were required to pay a premium comparable to that of civil employees, the net government outlay would be about JD 25 million.

Alternative assumptions of the uninsured population would produce different estimates. In particular, if the fraction of the population which is in the "no formal insurance" category is lower, all three cost measures would be smaller. Using 15 percent instead of 20 percent in the "no formal insurance" category would imply program costs of about JD 39 million, about JD 23 million as the increase in government outlays, and about JD 10 million of total national spending (see Attachment 3). Costs would also be lower if higher cost-sharing were charged under the new plan.

Social Security Coverage Mandate

A requirement that all employers arrange for coverage of their employees and dependents, and that all remaining uncovered persons arrange to buy coverage, would produce universal coverage similar to that produced by expanding the existing Civil Insurance Program, but with less cost to the government. Such an approach could take a variety of specific forms. Private health insurance could be the source of coverage for the newly insured, or government insurance could be sold at break-even rates. Employers could be required to pay for the entire cost of coverage for all workers and their dependents, or employers below specified sizes could be exempted, or employer contributions could be made less than the full cost of coverage, or classes of employees could be exempted (e.g., part time workers). Government subsidies could be offered for employers whose workers have wages below a certain threshold. Similar options exist for the individual side of the mandate.

Exhibit 6 shows the Future Law Profile matrix for one variation of this approach. All employees in firms with five or more employees without other formal coverage would be required to be covered through their employer. Coverage could be purchased from the MOH, but full costs (not the subsidized civil insurance rates) would be charged. Alternatively, employers could purchase coverage privately to satisfy the requirement.

Exhibit 6. Future Law Profile Matrix (1994) (JD Million) Population Group: Total					
		Type of Service			
Source of funds	*Total*	Inpatient Hospital	Primary Care	Drugs	Other
Total	346.9	121.9	91.8	100.0	33.2
Out-of-pocket	123.4	44.2	36.0	43.2	0.0
MOH	107.3	24.9	16.3	33.0	33.2
RMS	34.1	22.9	5.2	6.0	0.0
Other public	19.0.	6.6	4.5	7.9	0.0
Other private	63.1	23.3	29.8	10.0	0.0

Source: James Mays and Vivian Hon, World Bank, 1996.

Total program cost would be about JD 53 million, based on 1 million persons being subject to the mandate. The JD 23 million increase in government outlays would be smaller than in the expansion of Civil Insurance option because JD 9 million are assumed to be routed through newly purchased private coverage. This represents mandated spending where employers, confronted with arranging for unsubsidized coverage, opt to pay more for private coverage instead of buying coverage through the Civil Insurance Program. Premium collections would be much larger for the population enrolled in the Civil Insurance Program, leading to a net government spending increase of about JD 14 million.

Attachment 1: Health Expenditures

Table A1.1: Health Expenditures by Source of Payment (1989-1994) (JD Million)						
	1989	1990	1991	1992	1993	1994
Ministry of Health			59	62	84	93
Royal Medical Services			29	28	33	37
Other Public			15	19	21	25
Total Public	92	95	103	109	138	155
Private	94	90	123	138	156	177
Total	*186*	*185*	*226*	*247*	*294*	*332*

Source: Budgets from MOH, Health Insurance Directorate and JUH; Health Financing Study: Phase I.

Notes:

1.   Data for public sector for 1991-94 are actual expenditures - capital and recurrent -- obtained from the MOH, Health Insurance Directorate, RMS and JUH. Figures for UNRWA for the same period are from Health Financing Study: Phase I, p. 13

2.   Actual outlays and source of program breaks for 1989 and 1990 were not available due to the formulation of the National Medical Institute. Data were interpolated for the two years using the 1988 figure of 73.8 million JD (see Ellena and Preker, p. 3) and actual expenditure data from official sources for 1991.

3.   Estimation of private sector expenditures. 1994 figure for private sector was estimated using the methodology employed in Ellena and Preker (p. 17-20), modified as follows:

1.   Assume that 30 percent cross-over from the public sector to the private sector.
2.   Assume 90 percent of privately insured and 60 percent of uninsured are seeking care in the private sector.

Ellena and Preker assumed a ten percent crossover between public and private sector and vise versa. The 30 percent crossover is a revision upward. Based on observations and interviews, it appears that the crossovers are not symmetrical: (i) there is more crossover from the public to the private sector due to the higher perceived quality of care in the private facilities; and (ii) more of the uninsured would seek care in the public sector due to higher fees in the private sector.

The total number of clients in the private sector are estimated to be about 1.7 million. The total number of visits by type (generalists, specialists, home visits, OPD, surgery, delivery, cesarean and ward visits) are calculated using current client count times the 1988 ratios from Ellena and Preker.

Fees for each of these visits are adjusted for inflation by multiplying by the medical consumer price index (MCPI). In 1988, 65 percent of private sector expenditures were for pharmaceuticals.

(private sector consumes 85 percent of total spending on pharmaceuticals). In 1994, expenditures for pharmaceuticals are estimated to have been JD 63 million (80 percent of total spending on pharmaceuticals) and expenditures for medical supplies were JD 16 million (25 percent of pharmaceuticals).

4.   Real private expenditures for intervening years (1989-93) are interpolated using private sector expenditures, and accounting for annual change in patient days in the private sector.

Attachment 2: Coverage of Population

Figure A1.1 Coverage of the Population by Program, 1994

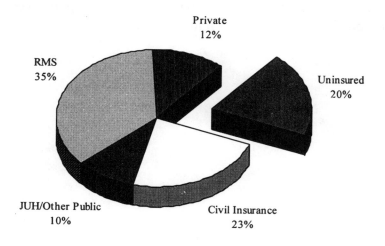

Source: J. Mays and V. Hon, "Health Financing Model for Jordan," from the November 1995 Mission to Jordan, World Bank, Washington, D.C., 1996.

1.   According to the Civil Insurance Program, 0.95 million people have been issued insurance cards, which include civil servants and their dependents (810,605); retirees and their dependents (51,197); poor and their dependents (88,022), disabled (4076) and blood donors (379) (Health Insurance Directorate statistics).

2.   The RMS covers 1.5 million people (Health Financing Study: Phase I, p. 22). This includes active and retired members of the Armed Forces, Public Security, Department of Intelligence, Department of Civil Defense and their dependents. In addition, the RMS also provides coverage to the Palestinian Liberation Army, the Royal Hashemite Court personnel, the Royal Jordanian Airlines, Aviation Academy and Arab Wings personnel and their dependents, and civilian personnel and students at Mu'ta University.

3.   Total number covered under "other public sector" includes JUH employees and 0.4 million Palestinian refugees covered under UNRWA (Health Financing Study: Phase I, p. 21).

4.   Assumed that 20 percent of population (800,000) have no insurance. This is consistent with information provided by Dr. Motasem Awamleh (General Director's Assistant for Financial Affairs, MOH) that 15-20 percent of people using MOH facilities have no insurance.

5.   Total number of privately insured from Health Financing Study: Phase 1 (p. 21) is defined as anyone without government insurance, which includes both the privately insured and the uninsured. The privately insured number here subtracts out the uninsured.

6.   Total number of people that have duplicate coverage is the gross coverage numbers (4.1 million) minus the total population (4.05 million).

7.   The net number of people covered is estimated by subtracting the gross coverage numbers for each of the program adjusted downward by the proportion covered under each of the programs multiplied by the duplicated number.

Attachment 3: Alternative Cost Scenarios for Providing Coverage through Civil Insurance

Table A1.2: Cost of Providing Coverage to the Uninsured through Civil Insurance

Expenditures (JD million)	Percent Uninsured		
	15	20	25
Current Law Total	332	332	332
Total Under Option	342	345	348
Current Law For Uninsured	32	43	54
Future Law For Uninsured	42	56	70
Change in Total	10	13	16
Change in Out of Pocket	-12	-17	-21
Change in MOH	22	30	37
Change in MOH Premiums	3	4	5
Net Change in MOH	19	26	32

Source: James Mays and Vivian Hon, World Bank, 1996.

ANNEX 2

JORDAN'S HEALTH SERVICE DELIVERY SYSTEM

Table A2.1: Education Programs for Health Personnel

Program	Location	Sponsor	Length in Years	Degree Granted	Graduates Per Year
Undergraduate Medical Schools:					
Jordan University Medical School (JU)	Amman	JU			110
Jordan University of Science and Technology (JUS	Irbid	JUST			40
Nursing Education:					
Rufeidah College of Nursing:	Amman	MOH	3	Diploma RN	200
Midwivery				Diploma MW	
Nuseibeh Mazenia Nursing and Midwifery College	Irbid	MOH	3	Diploma	100
Jordan University School of Nursing	Amman	JU	4	BS	
Jordan University School of Nursing	Amman	JU	2	MSN	8-10
Jordan University of Science & Technology	Irbid	JUST	4	BS	100
Princess Muna College of Nursing	Amman	RMS	3	Diploma	45-50
Midwivery			RN + 1		
Allied Health and Technical Schools:					
Clinical Teachers Training Institute	Al-Basheer, Amman	MOH		Diploma	15-20
Paramedical Institute	Irbid	MOH		Diploma	
RMS College for Allied Health Services	Marka	RMS	2	Diploma	
Medical Engineering Training Center	Amman	RMS/MOH	3	Diploma	

Source: **MOH, RMS, JUH.**

Table A2.2: Summary of Health Facilities and Services
Provided by All Sectors (1994)

Description	Number of Clinics	Number of Hospitals	Beds	Admissions	Patient Days	Occupancy Rate	Average Stay	Outpatient Visits
MINISTRY OF HEALTH:								
Hospitals	19	19	2,569	192,238	632,182	67.4%	3.3	1,382,166
Clinics:								
Comprehensive Health Centers	30		-					
Primary Care Centers	318							
Village Health Centers	258							
MCH Centers	268							
Dental Clinics	146							
Chest Disease Centers	11							
Subtotal: Clinics	1,050							4,648,066
ROYAL MEDICAL SERVICES:								
Hospitals	9	9	1,593	93,144	437,725	75.3%	4.7	1,708,676
Clinics:								
Health Centers	8							
Military Health Clinics	64							
Subtotal: Clinics	81							710,950
JORDAN UNIVERSITY HOSPITAL	1	1	461	19,663	90,235	53.6%	4.6	155,946
UNRWA: (Jordan)								
Health Units	20							
Dental Clinics	16							
Laboratories	13							
Specialist Clinics	8							
Diabetes Clinics	16							
Hypertension Clinics	11							
Subtotal: Clinics	84							1,432,972
SUBTOTAL: PUBLIC SECTOR	1,216	29	4,623	305,045	1,160,142	68.8%	3.8	10,038,776
PRIVATE SECTOR:								
Hospitals	36	36	1,997	146,437	354,976	48.7%	2.4	252,424
Clinics*	1,900							2,470,000
TOTAL: ALL SECTORS	3,152	65	6,620	451,482	1,515,118	62.7%	3.4	12,761,200

Source: MOH, RMS, JUH.

Table A2.3: Summary of Hospital Beds and Utilization (1988-1994)

Description	1988	1989	1990	1991	1992	1993	1994
Hospital Beds: Number							
Ministry of Health	2,268	2,169	2,223	2,223	2,359	2,372	2,569
Royal Medical Services	1,289	1,469	1,509	1,542	1,542	1,584	1,593
Jordan University Hospital	507	507	461	461	461	461	461
Private Sector	1,555	1,461	1,506	1,596	1,604	*1,800*	1,997
Total: Hospital Beds #	5,619	5,606	5,699	5,822	5,966	6,217	6,620
Hospital Beds: % of Total							
Ministry of Health	40.4%	38.7%	39.0%	38.2%	39.5%	38.2%	38.8%
Royal Medical Services	22.9%	26.2%	26.5%	26.5%	25.8%	25.5%	24.1%
Jordan University Hospital	9.0%	9.0%	8.1%	7.9%	7.7%	7.4%	7.0%
Private Sector	27.7%	26.1%	26.4%	27.4%	26.9%	29.0%	30.2%
Total: Hospital Beds %	100.0%	100.0%	100.0%	100.0%	100.0%	100.0%	100.0%
Admissions:							
Ministry of Health	142,517	150,029	145,477	149,116	161,175	179,872	192,238
Royal Medical Services	72,170	80,396	79,020	80,683	92,791	96,308	93,144
Jordan University Hospital	23,267	26,321	23,583	21,083	23,066	19,164	19,663
Private Sector	98,510	106,834	110,880	121,305	136,598	*141,517*	146,437
Total: Admissions	336,464	363,580	358,960	372,187	413,630	436,861	451,482
Patient Days:							
Ministry of Health	548,712	527,203	511,943	498,793	578,509	647,993	632,182
Royal Medical Services	356,522	379,080	384,717	356,139	425,533	452,286	437,725
Jordan University Hospital	132,860	131,552	119,382	96,192	112,206	90,748	90,235
Private Sector	246,275	260,766	*233,618*	*290,000*	*295,950*	*325,463*	354,976
Total: Patient Days	1,284,369	1,298,601	1,249,660	1,241,124	1,412,198	1,516,490	1,515,118
Occupancy Rate:							
Ministry of Health	66.1%	66.6%	63.1%	61.5%	67.0%	74.8%	67.4%
Royal Medical Services	75.6%	70.7%	69.8%	63.3%	75.4%	78.2%	75.3%
Jordan University Hospital	71.6%	71.1%	70.9%	57.2%	66.5%	53.9%	53.6%
Private Sector	43.3%	48.9%	42.5%	49.8%	50.4%	49.5%	48.7%
Total: Occupancy Rate	62.5%	63.5%	60.1%	58.4%	64.7%	66.8%	62.7%
Average Length of Stay:							
Ministry of Health	3.9	3.5	3.5	3.3	3.6	3.6	3.3
Royal Medical Services	4.9	4.7	4.9	4.4	4.6	4.7	4.7
Jordan University Hospital	5.7	5.0	5.1	4.6	4.9	4.7	4.6
Private Sector	2.5	2.4	2.1	2.4	2.2	2.3	2.4
Total: ALOS	3.8	3.6	3.5	3.3	3.4	3.5	3.4
Utilization Ratios:							
Population	2,940,318	3,053,000	3,170,000	3,545,000	3,733,000	3,888,000	4,035,000
Hospital Beds per 1,000	1.91	1.84	1.80	1.64	1.60	1.60	1.64
Admissions per 1,000	114.43	119.09	113.24	104.99	110.80	112.36	111.89
Patient Days per 1,000	436.81	425.35	394.21	350.11	378.30	390.04	375.49

Source: **MOH, RMS, JUH.**

Note: Data in italics are extrapolated.

Table A2.4: Hospital Beds and Utilization (1988)

#	Name	Location	Beds	Admissions	Patient Days	Occupancy Rate	Average Stay	Outpatient Visits
	MINISTRY OF HEALTH:							
1	Al-Basheer	Amman	514	34,141	149,538	79.5%	4.4	172,300
2	National Center of Psychiatry	Balqa	290	839	55,038	51.9%	65.6	37,856
3	Al-Karamah (Psychiatric with NCP)	Amman	94	251	30,750	89.4%	122.5	564
4	Al-Zarka	Zarka	260	18,695	57,945	60.9%	3.1	64,295
5	Princess Basma	Irbid	285	20,987	68,208	65.4%	3.3	197,118
	Princess Badea (OB/GYN)(Open '94)	Irbid	0					
6	Al-Hussein, Salt	Balqa	150	13,004	38,362	69.9%	3.0	54,554
7	Al-Mafraq	Mafraq	73	6,762	18,257	68.3%	2.7	39,746
8	Jarash	Jarash	75	5,063	17,721	64.6%	3.5	8,290
9	Al-Iman	Ajloun	82	5,711	13,706	45.7%	2.4	48,118
10	Ma'an	Ma'an	88	5,172	13,964	43.4%	2.7	0
11	Jamil Al-Toutanje	Madaba	72	6,721	20,161	76.5%	3.0	35,294
12	Al-Karak	Karak	80	6,979	24,427	83.4%	3.5	37,622
13	Al-Ramtha	Irbid	56	4,967	9,934	48.5%	2.0	59,168
14	Abu-Obaidah (JV North)	Irbid	32	2,542	8,389	71.6%	3.3	28,966
15	Al-Shuneh (JV South)	Balqa	29	2,122	4,244	40.0%	2.0	2,284
16	Mua'th Bin Jabal (JV North)	Irbid	31	2,689	5,378	47.4%	2.0	18,550
17	Ghor Al-Safi (JV South)	Karak	11	1,327	1,327	33.0%	1.0	3,738
	Al-Rueshid (Opened 1994)	Mafraq	0					
18	Tafilah (Closed 1992)	Tafilah	46	4,545	11,363	67.5%	2.5	29,436
18	SUB-TOTAL: MOH		2,268	142,517	548,712	66.1%	3.9	837,899
	ROYAL MEDICAL SERVICES:							
	King Hussein Medical Center:	Amman						
1	King Hussein Hospital		536	27,780	168,618	86.0%	6.1	115,944
2	Royal Jordanian Rehabilitation Centre		140	2,314	34,526	67.4%	14.9	16,800
3	Queen Alia Heart Institute		94	4,352	26,390	76.7%	6.1	10,196
	Queen Alia Military Hospital	Amman	0					
4	Prince Hashem Hospital	Zarka	180	10,474	39,374	59.8%	3.8	155,332
5	Prince Rashid Hospital	Irbid	200	16,704	56,034	76.5%	3.4	167,270
6	Princess Haya Hospital	Aqaba	70	5,580	15,724	61.4%	2.8	45,738
7	Prince Ali Hospital	Karak	69	4,966	15,856	62.8%	3.2	101,780
	Prince Zaid Hospital (Opened 1992)	Tafilah	0					
7	SUB-TOTAL: RMS		1,289	72,170	356,522	75.6%	4.9	613,060
1	*JORDAN UNIVERSITY HOSPITAL* *	Amman	507	23,267	132,860	71.6%	5.7	175,000
26	TOTAL: ALL PUBLIC HOSPITALS		4,064	237,954	1,038,094	69.3%	4.4	1,625,959
28	*PRIVATE HOSPITALS*		1,555	98,510	246,275	43.3%	2.5	130,624
54	TOTAL: ALL HOSPITALS		5,619	336,464	1,284,369	62.5%	3.8	1,756,583

Source: Ellena, G. and Preker, A., "Financing and Health Sector's Rehabilitation in Jordan," The World Bank: October 1, 1989.

Table A2.5 Hospital Beds and Utilization (1989)

#	Name	Location	Beds	Admissions	Patient Days	Occupancy Rate	Average Stay	Outpatient Visits
	MINISTRY OF HEALTH:							
1	Al-Basheer	Amman	519	35,164	152,154	80.3%	4.3	176,121
2	National Center of Psychiatry	Balqa	290	857	60,550	57.2%	70.7	39,280
3	Al-Karamah (Psychiatric with NCP)	Amman		-				568
4	Al-Zarka	Zarka	260	18,766	62,408	65.8%	3.3	144,339
5	Princess Basma	Irbid	278	24,740	69,376	68.4%	2.8	187,668
	Princess Badea (OB/GYN)(Open '94)	Irbid	0					
6	Al-Hussein, Salt	Balqa	150	13,549	31,107	56.8%	2.3	52,860
7	Al-Mafraq	Mafraq	73	6,772	16,063	60.3%	2.4	37,200
8	Jarash	Jarash	75	6,127	19,018	69.5%	3.1	52,546
9	Al-Iman	Ajloun	82	6,346	16,712	55.8%	2.6	47,462
10	Ma'an	Ma'an	86	4,889	16,372	52.2%	3.3	22,379
11	Jamil Al-Toutanje	Madaba	64	6,665	16,355	70.0%	2.5	39,920
12	Al-Karak	Karak	76	7,396	20,960	75.6%	2.8	37,275
13	Al-Ramtha	Irbid	56	5,495	12,067	59.0%	2.2	33,777
14	Abu-Obaidah (JV North)	Irbid	32	3,000	8,301	71.1%	2.8	24,885
15	Al-Shuneh (JV South)	Balqa	29	2,042	4,802	45.4%	2.4	4,759
16	Mua'th Bin Jabal (JV North)	Irbid	31	2,484	4,413	39.0%	1.8	17,796
17	Ghor Al-Safi (JV South)	Karak	22	1,389	4,407	54.9%	3.2	3,278
	Al-Rueshid (Opened 1994)	Mafraq	0					
18	Tafilah (Closed 1992)	Tafilah	46	4,348	12,138	72.3%	2.8	31,332
18	*SUB-TOTAL: MOH*		2,169	150,029	527,203	66.6%	3.5	953,445
	ROYAL MEDICAL SERVICES:							
	King Hussein Medical Center:	Amman						
1	King Hussein Hospital							
2	Royal Jordanian Rehabilitation Centre							
3	Queen Alia Heart Institute							
4	Queen Alia Military Hospital	Amman						
5	Prince Hashem Hospital	Zarka						
6	Prince Rashid Hospital	Irbid						
7	Princess Haya Hospital	Aqaba						
8	Prince Ali Hospital	Karak						
	Prince Zaid Hospital (Opened 11/92)	Tafileh						
8	*SUB-TOTAL: RMS*		1,469	80,396	379,080	70.7%	4.7	1,602,469
1	*JORDAN UNIVERSITY HOSPITAL*	Amman	507	26,321	131,552	71.1%	5.0	174,499
27	*TOTAL: ALL PUBLIC HOSPITALS*		4,145	256,746	1,037,835	68.6%	4.0	2,730,413
26	*PRIVATE HOSPITALS*		1,461	106,834	260,766	48.9%	2.4	143,963
53	*TOTAL: ALL HOSPITALS*		5,606	363,580	1,298,601	63.5%	3.6	2,874,376

Source: **MOH, RMS, JUH.**

Table A2.6 Hospital Beds and Utilization (1990)

#	Name	Location	Beds	Admissions	Patient Days	Occupancy Rate	Average Stay	Outpatient Visits
	MINISTRY OF HEALTH:							
1	Al-Basheer	Amman	529	34,893	149,342	77.3%	4.3	277,148
2	National Center of Psychiatry	Balqa	340	875	66,062	53.2%	75.5	50,925
3	Al-Karamah (Psychiatric with NCP)	Amman						
4	Al-Zarka	Zarka	260	18,807	62,063	65.4%	3.3	138,144
5	Princess Basma	Irbid	272	25,160	68,686	69.2%	2.7	160,990
	Princess Badea (OB/GYN)(Open '94)	Irbid	0					
6	Al-Hussein, Salt	Balqa	150	8,705	25,767	47.1%	3.0	57,211
7	Al-Mafraq	Mafraq	73	6,610	15,864	59.5%	.2.4	37,250
8	Jarash	Jarash	75	6,563	18,376	67.1%	2.8	48,741
9	Al-Iman	Ajloun	82	5,921	10,066	33.6%	1.7	32,227
10	Ma'an	Ma'an	86	5,188	17,639	56.2%	3.4	24,933
11	Jamil Al-Toutanje	Madaba	64	6,741	16,178	69.3%	2.4	44,537
12	Al-Karak	Karak	76	6,882	16,517	59.5%	2.4	49,766
13	Al-Ramtha	Irbid	56	5,929	10,672	52.2%	1.8	40,481
14	Abu-Obaidah (JV North)	Irbid	32	3,352	8,380	71.7%	2.5	36,323
15	Al-Shuneh (JV South)	Balqa	29	1,703	3,747	35.4%	2.2	8,002
16	Mua'th Bin Jabal (JV North)	Irbid	31	2,109	4,851	42.9%	2.3	27,587
17	Ghor Al-Safi (JV South)	Karak	22	2,207	6,620	82.4%	3.0	4,194
	Al-Rueshid (Opened 1994)	Mafraq	0					
18	Tafilah (Closed 1992)	Tafilah	46	3,832	*11,113*	66.2%	2.9	32,604
18	*SUB-TOTAL: MOH*		2,223	145,477	511,943	63.1%	3.5	1,071,063
	ROYAL MEDICAL SERVICES:							
	King Hussein Medical Center:	Amman						
1	King Hussein Hospital		564	28,944	171,435	83.3%	5.9	417,732
2	Royal Jordanian Rehabilitation Centre		140	2,387	30,309	59.3%	12.7	18,350
3	Queen Alia Heart Institute		94	4,708	26,960	78.6%	5.7	10,298
4	Queen Alia Military Hospital	Amman	169	7,073	35,285	57.2%	5.0	102,408
5	Prince Hashem Hospital	Zarka	180	11,064	40,702	62.0%	3.7	356,834
6	Prince Rashid Hospital	Irbid	200	13,618	45,696	62.6%	3.4	296,482
7	Princess Haya Hospital	Aqaba	77	5,772	18,621	66.3%	3.2	122,773
8	Prince Ali Hospital	Karak	85	5,454	15,709	50.6%	2.9	145,551
9	Prince Zaid Hospital (Opened 11/92)	Tafiieh	0					
9	*SUB-TOTAL: RMS*		1,509	79,020	384,717	69.8%	4.9	1,470,428
1	*JORDAN UNIVERSITY HOSPITAL*	Amman	461	23,583	119,382	70.9%	5.1	167,679
28	*TOTAL: ALL PUBLIC HOSPITALS*		4,193	248,080	1,016,042	66.4%	4.1	2,709,170
26	*PRIVATE HOSPITALS*		1,506	110,880	*233,618*	42.5%	2.1	157,894
54	*TOTAL: ALL HOSPITALS*		5,699	358,960	1,249,660	60.1%	3.5	2,867,064

Source: MOH, RMS, JUH.

Table A2.7: Hospital Beds and Utilization (1991)

#	Name	Location	Beds	Admissions	Patient Days	Occupancy Rate	Average Stay	Outpatient Visits
	MINISTRY OF HEALTH:							
1	Al-Basheer	Amman	529	33,247	142,962	74.0%	4.3	238,611
2	National Center of Psychiatry	Balqa	340	927	77,837	62.7%	84.0	58,336
3	Al-Karamah (Psychiatric with NCP)	Amman						0
4	Al-Zarka	Zarka	260	21,273	44,673	47.1%	2.1	169,671
5	Princess Basma	Irbid	272	24,103	65,078	65.5%	2.7	166,626
	Princess Badea (OB/GYN)(Open '94)	Irbid	0					0
6	Al-Hussein, Salt	Balqa	150	10,027	28,076	51.3%	2.8	62,517
7	Al-Mafraq	Mafraq	73	6,618	13,898	52.2%	2.1	38,342
8	Jarash	Jarash	75	7,606	20,536	75.0%	2.7	51,482
9	Al-Iman	Ajloun	82	5,700	10,260	34.3%	1.8	54,751
10	Ma'an	Ma'an	86	4,911	18,662	59.5%	3.8	25,845
11	Jamil Al-Toutanje	Madaba	64	6,969	16,029	68.6%	2.3	45,741
12	Al-Karak	Karak	76	7,197	15,114	54.5%	2.1	42,985
13	Al-Ramtha	Irbid	56	6,227	11,209	54.8%	1.8	41,025
14	Abu-Obaidah (JV North)	Irbid	32	3,509	9,123	78.1%	2.6	37,487
15	Al-Shuneh (JV South)	Balqa	29	1,932	3,671	34.7%	1.9	7,684
16	Mua'th Bin Jabal (JV North)	Irbid	31	2,126	4,039	35.7%	1.9	26,745
17	Ghor Al-Safi (JV South)	Karak	22	2,789	8,925	111.1%	3.2	6,687
	Al-Rueshid (Opened 1994)	Mafraq	0					0
18	Tafilah (Closed 1992)	Tafilah	46	3955	8701	51.8%	2.2	0
18	SUB-TOTAL: MOH		2,223	149,116	498,793	61.5%	3.3	1,074,535
	ROYAL MEDICAL SERVICES:							
	King Hussein Medical Center:	Amman						
1	King Hussein Hospital		564	27,521	154,324	75.0%	5.6	467,606
2	Royal Jordanian Rehabilitation Centre		137	2,281	28,975	57.9%	12.7	17,679
3	Queen Alia Heart Institute		100	4,619	25,946	71.1%	5.6	8,912
4	Queen Alia Military Hospital	Amman	194	6,368	28,048	39.6%	4.4	74,888
5	Prince Hashem Hospital	Zarka	182	13,019	38,352	57.7%	2.9	370,343
6	Prince Rashid Hospital	Irbid	200	15,818	48,060	65.8%	3.0	394,710
7	Princess Haya Hospital	Aqaba	84	5,455	14,755	48.1%	2.7	139,405
8	Prince Ali Hospital	Karak	81	5,602	17,679	59.8%	3.2	156,459
9	Prince Zaid Hospital (Opened 11/92)	Tafileh	0					
9	SUB-TOTAL: RMS		1,542	80,683	356,139	63.3%	4.4	1,630,002
1	*JORDAN UNIVERSITY HOSPITAL*	Amman	461	21,083	96,192	57.2%	4.6	141,036
28	*TOTAL: ALL PUBLIC HOSPITALS*		4,226	250,882	951,124	61.7%	3.8	2,845,573
28	*PRIVATE HOSPITALS*		1,596	121,305	290,000	49.8%	2.4	196,042
56	*TOTAL: ALL HOSPITALS*		5,822	372,187	1,241,124	58.4%	3.3	3,041,615

Source: MOH, RMS, JUH.

Table A2.8: Hospital Beds and Utilization (1992)

#	Name	Location	Beds	Admissions	Patient Days	Occupancy Rate	Average Stay	Outpatient Visits
	MINISTRY OF HEALTH:							
1	Al-Basheer	Amman	619	35,461	159,574	70.4%	4.5	300,806
2	National Center of Psychiatry	Balqa	365	979	89,612	67.1%	91.5	70,280
3	Al-Karamah (Psychiatric with NCP)	Amman		-				
4	Al-Zarka	Zarka	260	22,018	63,852	67.1%	2.9	189,570
5	Princess Basma	Irbid	280	26,859	83,263	81.2%	3.1	174,882
	Princess Badea (OB/GYN)(Open '94)	Irbid	0					0
6	Al-Hussein, Salt	Balqa	150	12,881	34,778	63.3%	2.7	79,522
7	Al-Mafraq	Mafraq	120	7,901	19,752	45.0%	2.5	46,011
8	Jarash	Jarash	87	8,676	19,955	62.7%	2.3	58,031
9	Al-Iman	Ajloun	82	6,719	14,110	47.0%	2.1	59,172
10	Ma'an	Ma'an	86	6,108	18,324	58.2%	3.0	28,650
11	Jamil Al-Toutanje	Madaba	64	7,929	18,237	77.9%	2.3	52,165
12	Al-Karak	Karak	76	8,075	16,150	58.1%	2.0	51,852
13	Al-Ramtha	Irbid	56	7,540	13,572	66.2%	1.8	47,739
14	Abu-Obaidah (JV North)	Irbid	32	3,777	9,443	80.6%	2.5	37,380
15	Al-Shuneh (JV South)	Balqa	29	2,114	4,651	43.8%	2.2	9,609
16	Mua'th Bin Jabal (JV North)	Irbid	31	2,447	4,894	43.1%	2.0	25,865
17	Ghor Al-Safi (JV South)	Karak	22	2,691	8,342	103.6%	3.1	8,229
	Al-Rueshid (Opened 1994)	Mafraq	0					0
	Tafilah (Closed 1992)	Tafilah	0					0
17	*SUB-TOTAL: MOH*		2,359	162,175	578,509	67.0%	3.6	1,239,763
	ROYAL MEDICAL SERVICES:							
	King Hussein Medical Center:	Amman						
1	King Hussein Hospital		564	27,912	179,321	86.9%	6.4	494,683
2	Royal Jordanian Rehabilitation Centre		137	2,603	33,531	66.9%	12.9	32,272
3	Queen Alia Heart Institute		100	4,959	28,775	78.6%	5.8	9,022
4	Queen Alia Military Hospital	Amman	194	8,987	40,217	56.6%	4.5	74,676
5	Prince Hashem Hospital	Zerka	182	13,069	44,560	66.9%	3.4	375,962
6	Prince Rashid Hospital	Irbid	200	19,780	60,499	82.6%	3.1	420,172
7	Princess Haya Hospital	Aqaba	84	6,284	17,914	58.3%	2.9	156,706
8	Prince Ali Hospital	Kerak	81	9,197	20,716	69.9%	2.3	154,344
	Prince Zaid Hospital (Opened 11/92)	Tafileh	0					
8	*SUB-TOTAL: RMS*		1,542	92,791	425,533	75.4%	4.6	1,717,837
1	*JORDAN UNIVERSITY HOSPITAL*	Amman	461	23,066	112,206	66.5%	4.9	158,289
26	*TOTAL: ALL PUBLIC HOSPITALS*		4,362	278,032	1,116,248	69.9%	4.0	3,115,889
28	*PRIVATE HOSPITALS*		1,604	136,598	295,950	50.4%	2.2	240,626
54	*TOTAL: ALL HOSPITALS*		5,966	414,630	1,412,198	64.7%	3.4	3,356,515

Source: **MOH, RMS, JUH.**

Table A2.9: Hospital Beds and Utilization (1993)

#	Name	Location	Beds	Admissions	Patient Days	Occupancy Rate	Average Stay	Outpatient Visits
	MINISTRY OF HEALTH:							
1	Al-Basheer	Amman	647	41,832	188,895	80.0%	4.5	303,155
2	National Center of Psychiatry	Balqa	329	1,031	101,388	84.4%	98.3	51,049
3	Al-Karamah (Psychiatric with NCP)	Amman						
4	Al-Zarka	Zarka	260	23,687	67,623	71.3%	2.9	187,341
5	Princess Basma	Irbid	276	28,097	76,226	75.7%	2.7	223,396
	Princess Badea (OB/GYN)(Open '94)	Irbid	0					0
6	Al-Hussein, Salt	Balqa	140	14,257	37,443	73.3%	2.6	77,945
7	Al-Mafraq	Mafraq	132	10,479	31,553	65.5%	3.0	59,163
8	Jarash	Jarash	88	9,029	21,189	66.0%	2.3	72,456
9	Al-Iman	Ajloun	82	8,242	16,147	53.9%	2.0	66,609
10	Ma'an	Ma'an	86	6,693	21,842	69.6%	3.3	33,320
11	Jamil Al-Toutanje	Madaba	70	8,645	20,311	79.5%	2.3	58,141
12	Al-Karak	Karak	76	7,824	21,481	77.4%	2.7	59,843
13	Al-Ramtha	Irbid	56	7,789	14,648	71.7%	1.9	49,214
14	Abu-Obaidah (JV North)	Irbid	32	3,968	9,663	82.7%	2.4	37,102
15	Al-Shuneh (JV South)	Balqa	34	2,572	5,498	44.3%	2.1	13,546
16	Mua'th Bin Jabal (JV North)	Irbid	31	2,820	5,608	49.6%	2.0	24,696
17	Ghor Al-Safi (JV South)	Karak	33	2,907	8,478	70.4%	2.9	10,439
18	Al-Rueshid (Opened 1994)	Mafraq	0					0
	Tafilah (Closed 1992)	Tafilah	0					0
18	*SUB-TOTAL: MOH*		2,372	179,872	647,993	74.8%	3.6	1,327,415
	ROYAL MEDICAL SERVICES:							
	King Hussein Medical Center:	Amman						
1	King Hussein Hospital		564	28,045	185,833	90.3%	6.6	347,330
2	Royal Jordanian Rehabilitation Centre		137	2,557	31,985	64.0%	12.5	33,270
3	Queen Alia Heart Institute		100	4,897	28,778	78.8%	5.9	10,878
4	Queen Alia Military Hospital	Amman	194	10,468	45,681	64.5%	4.4	85,120
5	Prince Hashem Hospital	Zarka	182	12,148	44,296	66.7%	3.6	432,510
6	Prince Rashid Hospital	Irbid	200	21,327	63,487	87.0%	3.0	432,994
7	Princess Haya Hospital	Aqaba	84	5,825	18,908	61.7%	3.2	129,016
8	Prince Ali Hospital	Karak	81	5,828	18,816	63.6%	3.2	164,947
9	Prince Zaid Hospital (Opened 1992)	Tafileh	42	5,213	14,502	94.6%	2.8	83,816
9	*SUB-TOTAL: RMS*		1,584	96,308	452,286	78.2%	4.7	1,719,881
1	*JORDAN UNIVERSITY HOSPITAL*	Amman	461	19,164	90,748	53.9%	4.7	145,281
28	*TOTAL: ALL PUBLIC HOSPITALS*		4,417	295,344	1,191,027	73.9%	4.0	3,192,577
32	*PRIVATE HOSPITALS*		*1,800*	*141,517*	*325,463*	*49.5%*	*2.3*	*246,525*
60	*TOTAL: ALL HOSPITALS*		6,217	436,861	1,516,490	66.8%	3.5	3,439,102

Source: MOH, RMS, JUH.

Table A2.10: Hospital Beds and Utilization (1994)

#	Name	Location	Beds	Admissions	Patient Days	Occupancy Rate	Average Stay	Outpatient Visits
	MINISTRY OF HEALTH:							
1	Al-Basheer	Amman	672	46,270	203,843	83.1%	4.4	356,460
2	National Center of Psychiatry	Balqa	280	1,270	62,040	60.7%	48.9	20,475
3	Al-Karamah (Psychiatric with NCP)	Amman						2,708
4	Al-Zarka	Zarka	268	25,808	69,823	71.4%	2.7	205,399
5	Princess Basma	Irbid	204	11,955	44,878	60.3%	3.8	203,040
6	Princess Badea (OB/GYN)(Open '94)	Irbid	200	17,216	43,441	59.5%	2.5	29,805
7	Al-Hussein, Salt	Balqa	140	13,587	36,850	72.1%	2.7	73,581
8	Al-Mafraq	Mafraq	138	11,307	32,091	63.7%	2.8	59,055
9	Jarash	Jarash	125	9,974	20,999	46.0%	2.1	64,961
10	Al-Iman	Ajloun	97	8,824	15,931	45.0%	1.8	64,480
11	Ma'an	Ma'an	86	8,321	17,435	55.5%	2.1	33,147
12	Jamil Al-Toutanje	Madaba	78	9,631	20,758	72.9%	2.2	64,197
13	Al-Karak	Karak	76	7,701	20,903	75.4%	2.7	53,665
14	Al-Ramtha	Irbid	56	7,493	14,921	73.0%	2.0	54,698
15	Abu-Obaidah (JV North)	Irbid	35	3,666	8,124	63.6%	2.2	38,407
16	Al-Shuneh (JV South)	Balqa	34	2,634	4,708	37.9%	1.8	13,745
17	Mua'th Bin Jabal (JV North)	Irbid	33	3,025	5,801	48.2%	1.9	27,636
18	Ghor Al-Safi (JV South)	Karak	33	2,910	8,717	72.4%	3.0	12,899
19	Al-Rueshid (Opened 1994)	Mafraq	14	646	919	18.0%	1.4	3,808
	Tafilah (Closed 1992)	Tafilah	0					
19	*SUB-TOTAL: MOH*		2,569	192,238	632,182	67.4%	3.3	1,382,166
	ROYAL MEDICAL SERVICES:							
	King Hussein Medical Center:	Amman						
1	King Hussein Hospital		564	24,045	177,703	86.3%	7.4	390,737
2	Royal Jordanian Rehabilitation Centre		130	2,580	32,485	68.5%	12.6	34,375
3	Queen Alia Heart Institute		100	5,135	28,568	78.3%	5.6	14,989
4	Queen Alia Military Hospital	Amman	194	11,089	46,817	66.1%	4.2	87,312
5	Prince Hashem Hospital	Zarka	182	11,631	41,098	61.9%	3.5	377,148
6	Prince Rashid Hospital	Irbid	200	22,054	61,283	83.9%	2.8	409,848
7	Princess Haya Hospital	Aqaba	84	6,024	19,141	62.4%	3.2	117,311
8	Prince Ali Hospital	Karak	79	5,395	16,407	56.9%	3.0	181,044
9	Prince Zaid Hospital (Opened 11/92)	Tafileh	60	5,191	14,243	65.0%	2.7	95,912
9	*SUB-TOTAL: RMS*		1,593	93,144	437,745	75.3%	4.7	1,708,676
1	*JORDAN UNIVERSITY HOSPITAL*	Amman	461	19,663	90,235	53.6%	4.6	155,946
29	*TOTAL: ALL PUBLIC HOSPITALS*		4,623	305,045	1,160,162	68.8%	3.8	3,246,788
36	*PRIVATE HOSPITALS*		1,997	146,437	354,976	48.7%	2.4	252,424
65	*TOTAL: ALL HOSPITALS*		6,620	451,482	1,515,138	62.7%	3.4	3,499,212

Source: **MOH, RMS, JUH.**

ANNEX 3

OVERVIEW OF JORDAN'S HEALTH CARE SYSTEM

Eligibility

- Civil servants and their families (23 percent of the population) pay limited premiums to receive coverage under the Civil Insurance System and receive care in primary care centers run by the MOH and MOH hospitals.

- Individuals certified as poor (as well as the disabled and blood donors) by the authorities are also covered under the Civil Insurance System and receive free (primary and hospital) as well as subsidized services (pharmaceuticals) in MOH facilities

- Military and their dependents (35 percent of the population) pay very limited premiums and receive care in MOH primary care centers and Royal Medical Services (RMS) hospitals.

- Jordan University Hospital covers its employees and dependents (0.5 percent of the population) and is also a major fee-for-service referral center.

- A private health Insurance system operates via large firms either self-insuring or purchasing private health insurance from private insurance companies for their employees (covers 12 percent of the population)

- United Nations Relief Works Agency (UNRWA) provides coverage to some 400,000 Palestinian refugees.

- The Social Security Corporation financed by payroll tax contributions from employers and employees in firms of 5 employees or more finances retirement pensions, disability allowances, and work-related accident and injury medical expenses. While the Law also provides for contribution-based health insurance (Article 3.A.4), this section of the Law has not been implemented.

- An estimated 20 percent of the population, many near-poor who work for the government, self-employed, and individuals employed in firms which do not offer insurance to their employees, have no formal coverage, can pay out-of-pocket fees and receive highly subsidized care in MOH facilities.

Benefits

- Free primary (physician, lab, and diagnostic) and hospital care in MOH facilities (or RMS facilities for military-related) for civil servants, military, and poor.

- Drugs are subsidized for these groups with the military-related individuals getting the largest subsidies.

- Civil servants and poor who seek treatment outside their assigned zone are treated as uninsured.

- Benefits offered by private firms are quite variable and frequently have copayments, deductibles and exclusions.

Financing (Sources of Revenue)

- The MOH system is financed from the general budget, small premium contributions by civil servants and out-of-pocket payments for drugs and out of zone services and fees from the uninsured.

- The RMS system is financed from the Defense Ministry Budget, small(er) premium contributions, copayments for pharmaceuticals, and fees.

- Private insurance is financed by employer contributions, employee premiums, and out-of-pocket payments depending on the specifics of the policy.

- UNRWA is funded by outside donor assistance.

- JUH is funded through budget allocations and fees.

Reimbursement of Medical Care Providers

- MOH facilities are paid directly via the MOH budget and through fees from the uninsured based on a schedule established by the MOH.

- RMS facilities are paid via the Defense Ministry Budget and fees.

- MOH and RMS facilities do not have individual facility budgets, rather all moneys and supplies are allocated centrally by the MOH and RMS.

- Physicians and other public facility staff are salaried public employees.

- Private practitioners and facilities are generally paid on a fee-for-service basis, although other contractual relationships may exist.

Delivery System

- The MOH runs a very extensive primary care system (e.g., 1050 facilities and branches) for basically all individuals composed of village health centers, maternal and child health centers, primary care health centers, dental clinics, and comprehensive community health centers.

- UNRWA operates primary care centers and specialized clinics for refugees.

- There are 65 hospitals in Jordan including 19 MOH hospitals (39 percent of beds), 9 RMS hospitals (24 percent), the JUH (7 percent), and 36 private hospitals (30 percent).

- There are 1.6 hospital beds per 1000 population.

- In terms of manpower per 1000 population, Jordan has 1.6 physicians, 0.45 dentists, 0.75 pharmacists, 0.93 nurses, 0.2 midwifes, 1.1 assistant and 0.8 practical nurses.

- There is little planning regarding equipment and manpower.

- There is little coordination among the separate MOH, RMS, JUH, and private delivery systems.

- Public health programs are generally well targeted at individual infectious diseases, but not chronic conditions.

- Regulation of private sector insurers and providers is quite limited.

- Pharmaceuticals are procured through four separate public programs and the private sector, and there is no essential drugs list.

- Most pharmaceuticals are readily available.

References

Al-Khasawneh, S., <u>Distribution of Income from Wages Among Private Sector Workers Who are Subject to Social Security Regulations in Jordan</u>, Ministry of Labour, 1988.

Al-Qutob, R. and Mawajdeh, S., "Assessment of the Quality of Prenatal Care: The Transmission of Information to Pregnant Women in Maternal and Child Health Centers in Jordan," <u>International Quarterly of Community Health Education</u>, Vol 13(1), pgs. 47-62, 1992-93.

American Academy of Actuaries, "Medical Savings Accounts: Cost Implications and Design Issues," May 1995.

Australian Health Insurance Commission; <u>Turkey Health Financing Policy Options Study: Summary Report</u>; Ankara, 1995.

Berki, S., <u>Hospital Economics</u>, Lexington Books, Lexington, Massachusettes, 1972.

Berman, P. et. al., <u>Egypt: Strategies for Health Sector Change</u> (draft paper), Harvard University, Boston, August 1995.

Birch and Davis International, Inc., <u>Feasibility of Restructuring the Health Care Financing System in Jordan</u>, Prepared for USAID, 1989.

Bobadilla, J.L. et al., "The Epidemiological Transition and Health Priorities," in D. Jamison et al. (eds) <u>Disease Control Priorities in Developing Countries</u>, Oxford University Press, New York, 1993.

Bos E., "Demographic Trends in Jordan," Report from the November 1995 Mission to Jordan, World Bank, Washington, D.C., 1995.

Center for Consultation, Technical Services and Studies, <u>Health Financing Study Phase I: Universal Health Insurance Study</u>, Submitted to the World Bank, Amman, Jordan, University of Jordan, March 1995.

Center for Consultation, Technical Services and Studies, <u>Application of Health Insurance Schemes for Participants in the Social Security System</u>, University of Jordan, Amman, Jordan, 1994.

Center for International Health Information, 1994 Country Health Profile: <u>Jordan Health Situation and Statistics Report</u>, 1994.

Central Bank of Jordan, <u>Monthly Statistical Bulletin</u>, various issues, Department of Research and Studies, Jordan.

Cole, H., Smith, R. and Sukkary, S., <u>Pharmacists, Pharmacies, and the Pharmaceutical Sector in Jordan: Implications for Basic Health Care</u>, Prepared for USAID, Washington, DC, Futures Group, 1983.

Cowley, P. and Claeson, M., "Public Health Interventions and Cost Effectiveness," Report from the November 1995 Mission to Jordan, World Bank, Washington, D.C., 1996.

Currie, J., "Socio-Economic Status and Child Health: Does Public Health Insurance Narrow the Gap?" Scandinavian Journal of Economics, 97(4), 1995.

"Demographic and Health Survey Newsletter," Vol. 7, No. 2, Macro International Inc., 1995.

Doorslaer, E. V., A. Wagstaff and F. Rutten, Equity in the Finance and Delivery of Health Care, Oxford University Press, Oxford, 1993.

Egypt Ministry of Health and Harvard Data for Decision-Making Project, "National Health Accounts in Egypt," Harvard University, Boston, 1995.

Ellena, G. and Preker, A., "Financing the Health Sector's Rehabilitation in Jordan," the World Bank, Washington, D.C., 1989.

Ferster, G. and Goodhope, S., An Economic, Financial and Organizational Prefeasibility Framework for Developing a Comprehensive National Insurance System for the Hashemite Kingdom of Jordan, United States Agency for International Development and the Westinghouse Applied Public System Project, 1985.

Gornick, M. et al., "U.S. Initiatives and Approaches for Outcomes and Effectiveness Research," Health Policy, 17 (1991).

Hashemite Kingdom of Jordan, The Social Security Law, Provisional Law No. 30 of 1978.

Homedes, N., "The Disability Adjusted Life Year (DALY) - Definition, Measurement and Potential Use"; Human Capital Development Working Paper No. 68; World Bank, July 1996.

Hopkinson, M., "Health Sector Study Mission: Buildings and Equipment," Report from the November 1995 Mission to Jordan, World Bank, Washington, D.C., 1996.

International Monetary Fund, Macroeconomy of the Middle East and North Africa Exploiting Potential for Growth and Financial Stability, IMF, Washington, D.C., October 1995.

Jordanian Association for Family Planning and Protection (JAFPP), Strategic Plan 1994-2000.

Kelley, A. and Schmidt, R., "Aggregate Population and Economic Growth Correlations: The Role of the Components of Demographic Change," Demography, November 1995.

Kharabsheh, A. A., Health Care Expenditures and their Impact on Different Income Groups, Draft paper prepared for the Workshop on Income Distribution and Its Social Impact in Jordan, 1988.

Luft, H., "Health Maintenance Organizations: Is the United States Experience Applicable Elsewhere?" Health: Quality and Choice, OECD, Paris, 1994.

Mah, Samy El-Banna, Technical Assistance in Jordan Review of Health Needs and Health Services, (Trip Report #1), Prepared for the World Bank, Washington, D.C., 1989.

The Medical Consultants Corporation, <u>Health Insurance Project for the Private Sector</u>, Presented to Business Owners from the Private Sector, 1988.

Ministry of Health

_____1995, "Health Insurance for Jordanian Pre-School Children," unpublished memo.

_____1995, Data supplement to Health Financing Study.

_____1994, <u>Statistical Yearbook</u>, Hashemite Kingdom of Jordan.

_____1993, <u>Promotion, Protection and Regulation Safety of Food, Water and Drug in Jordan</u>.

_____1993, "Health Facility Survey," Disease Control Directorate/CDD Programme in Collaboration with WHO and UNICEF,

_____1992, <u>Jordan Population and Family Health Survey, 1990</u>, Ministry of Health, Amman, Jordan, August 1992, p.79.

_____1991, "Assessment of the Nutritional Status of Pre-School Children in Jordan."

_____1990, <u>Demographic and Health Survey</u>.

Murray, C. et al, "National Health Expenditures: A Global Analysis," in C. Murray and A. Lopez (eds.), <u>Global Comparative Assessments in the Health Sector</u>, WHO, Geneva, 1994.

Musgrove, P., "Public and Private Roles in Health: Theory and Financing Patterns," <u>Discussion Paper</u>, World Bank, Washington, D.C., February 1996.

Musgrove, P., "Measurement of Equity in Health," <u>World Health Statistics</u>, 39(4), 1986.

Newhouse, J., "Reimbursement Under Uncertainty: What to Do if One Cannot Identify An Efficient Hospital," Report prepared for the U.S. Health Care Financing Administration, Baltimore, 1993.

Obemeyer, C. M., and Potter, J., "Maternal Health Care Utilization in Jordan: A Study of Patterns and Determinants," <u>Studies in Family Planning</u>, 22, 3: 177-87, 1991.

OECD

_____1995, <u>New Directions in Health Policy</u>, OECD, Paris.

_____1995, Eco Sante Database, OECD, Paris.

_____1994, <u>The Reform of Health Care Systems: A Review of Seventeen Countries</u>, OECD, Paris.

OECD (continued)

_____1992, The Reform of Health Care: A Comparative Analysis of Seven OECD Countries, OECD, Paris.

"Oman - Child Health Survey," Ministry of Health, 1992.

"Qatar - Child Health Survey," Ministry of Health, Qatar, 1991.

Schieber, G. et al., "Health System Performance in OECD Countries," Health Affairs, Summer, 1994.

Schieber, G., "Preconditions for Health Reform: Experiences From the OECD Countries," Health Policy, (32), 1995.

Siegfried, R. J., Study on Health Insurance Scheme, United Nations Development Programme, 1991.

Taylor, R., "Health Services Organization and Management," Report from the November 1995 World Bank Mission to Jordan, World Bank, Washington, D.C., 1995.

"The National Population Strategy for Jordan" (draft), The National Population Commission, 1995.

"The National Strategy for Women in Jordan," The Jordanian National Committee for Women, 1993.

UNICEF

_____1995, State of the World's Children.

_____1992, Situation Analysis of Jordanian Children and Women.

U.S. Department of State, Bureau of Public Affairs, Background Notes on Jordan, 1995.

World Health Organization

_____1994, "Diarrhoeal Disease Control (CDD) Programme," Weekly Epidemiological Record, no. 18, May 6, 1994.

_____1993, Regional Office for the Eastern Mediterranean, Report of the Joint Government/WHO Programme Review Mission.

_____1992, The Work of WHO in the Eastern Mediterranean Region, Annual Report of the Regional Director.

_____1987, Jordan: Evaluation of the Strategy for Health for All by the Year 2000, Seventh Report on the World Situation, Vol. 6.

_____List of Indicators for the Health for All by the Year 2000.

World Bank

_____1996, "Jordan Country Brief," World Bank, Washington, D.C., February 1996.

_____1995, "Jordan: Country Assistance Strategy," World Bank, Washington, D.C., September 8, 1995.

_____1995, Claiming the Future: Choosing Prosperity in the Middle East and North Africa, Washington, D.C.

_____1995, Peace and the Jordanian Economy, Washington, D.C.

_____1995, World Development Report 1995: Workers in an Integrating World. .New York, Oxford University Press.

_____1995, Social Indicators of Development, Washington, D.C.

_____1994, Hashemite Kingdom of Jordan: Poverty Assessment, The World Bank, Washington, D.C.

_____1994, "Country Economic Report: Consolidating Economic Adjustment and Establishing the Basis for Sustainable Growth," Washington, D.C.

_____1994, Report on Jordan's Insurance Sector, Washington, D.C.

_____1994, Fertility in Jordan, Washington, D.C.

_____1994, Jordan Primary Health Care Project, Project Completion Report. Washington, D.C.

_____1993, World Development Report: Investing in Health, New York: Oxford University Press.

_____1993, Hashemite Kingdom of Jordan, Health Management Project, Staff Appraisal Report (SAR) Washington, D.C.

_____1990, Hashemite Kingdom of Jordan, Health Sector Development Project, SAR Washington, D.C.

_____1989, Quality, Organization and Finance Issues in the Health Sector, Washington, D.C.

_____1989, Study on Financing of Health Needs in Jordan, Washington, D.C.

_____1984, Jordan Health Sector Review, Population, Health and Nutrition Department. Washington, D.C.

_____Economic and Social Database

_____(memo) Economic Parameters for Project Analysis, Washington, D.C.

Worzala, C., The Demographic Dimensions of Poverty in Jordan, Washington, D.C., 1994.

Zou'bi, A. A. A. et. al Jordan Population and Family Survey, IRD/Macro International Inc., Columbia, Maryland, 1990.